Leading the Family of God

Library of Congress Cataloging in Publication Data

Miller, Paul M.
    Leading the family of God.

    Includes bibliographical references.
    1. Pastoral theology. I. Title.
BV4011.M496   253   81-2267
ISBN 0-8361-1950-9 (pbk.)   AACR2

Scripture quotations are from the Revised Standard Version of the Bible, copyrighted 1946, 1952, © 1971, 1973 or are the author's own paraphrase.

LEADING THE FAMILY OF GOD
Copyright © 1981 by Herald Press, Scottdale, Pa. 15683
    Published simultaneously in Canada by Herald Press,
    Kitchener, Ont. N2G 4M5
Library of Congress Catalog Card Number: 81-2267
International Standard Book Number: 0-8361-1950-9
Printed in the United States of America
Design: Alice B. Shetler

81 82 83 84 85 86 10 9 8 7 6 5 4 3 2 1

I dedicate this book to the members of my cluster in the Belmont congregation who seek to be "the family of God" for Bertha and me—

by fellowship which makes our heavenly Father real
by helping to discern our gifts for ministry
by sharing in major decisions we need to make
by welcoming our counsel in decisions they make
by caring what happens to us
by providing intergenerational recreation and fun
by praying for us.

Contents

Appendixes

Introduction

Is the church a mini-corporation? A model democracy? A community of learning? An AA-type support community for sinners? A hospital for dependent people with a thoroughly professional staff? Or a family of families knit together as the family of God?

The model assumed shapes the style of life lived, determines the values to be prioritized, defines the way power, leadership, and decision-making will proceed.

Out of years of ministry as a layperson, pastor, bishop, educator, chaplain, supervisor, consultant, leadership team member, mediator, therapist, Paul Miller affirms the familial model as the central biblical, theological, and practical understanding of the living church.

This is no outdated image or obsolete metaphor from centuries past. It is as contemporary as a church board meeting, a worship service, a pastoral call. When the church exists as a community of the Spirit, it is an extended family, a family of families which forms a network of relationships, covenants, loyalties, and joint commitments to witness, service, and faithfulness.

An organism rather than an organization, the church is a community of persons discovering personhood in brother-sisterhood. An interlinking network of sibling relationships the church functions, when healthy, as a family system with distributed power, shared functions of leadership, horizontal rather than vertical communication patterns, fraternal rather than professional relationships. This is obviously a reversal of hierarchical pyramidal organizational development and a choice of the organismic systems understanding as most appropriate to carrying out the teachings of Jesus.

Writing from within the believers' church tradition, Miller sees the voluntariness of the church as crucial. When inclusion is a matter of choice, power is exercised in equal respect for each person's responsibility and affection is shared out of equal regard for all others.

Voluntariness is central.

Voluntary membership is admission by choice. Born into the family of God, one must achieve a separate identity and then choose to reunite with the family or community by inner direction.

Voluntary covenanting is commitment to life with one another by personal choice.

Voluntary discipleship is an inner motivation to serve, risk, and work out obedience in life.

Voluntary disciplines for self-correction and direction, for challenge and invitation, bid the whole body to grow.

Voluntary centering in the Word and Spirit, in worship and fellowship, provides a vital core.

Voluntary aid offers mutual sharing, material help in times of need, and redistribution of goods to use possessions creatively.

In the healthy family system all of these are experienced as truly voluntary. In the fused or frozen family, they become oppressive obligations. Personal power is usurped by the collective. Freedom, choice, and responsivity are diminished. It is the healthy family system as a dynamic, balanced, and maturing whole which Miller uses as the central motif for congregational life in the believers' church. It is this balance of wholeness in health that he seeks to safeguard, to utilize for authenticity together and faithfulness in the world.

The clarity of application, aptness of illustration, tentativeness with rule-building, yet frankness in offering counsel, all unite to commend this volume to lay leader, elder, or pastor for reflection and direction of ministry in the church as the family of God.

David Augsburger
Associated Mennonite Biblical Seminaries
Elkhart, Indiana, March 1981

Author's Preface

In this book I take seriously God's call to Christians to be His children, His sons and daughters, and to relate to one another as members of His family.

In various ways I seek to apply the model of family life to congregational life. I feel that the closeness, the belonging, the interdependence, and the deep sense of identity as God's children could be greatly increased in congregations if members would consciously relate to each other, structure their lives, and decide things more like a family—and less like a corporation or a country club.

I review specific actions which leaders can do as they administer the life of the congregation to help God's children celebrate, support one another, back each other, share, keep one another informed, manage their money, and give each other feedback like a family.

However, I do not recommend the *Bruderhof* model. I do not suggest that all members of God's family have one common treasury, or that they live together in one settlement or compound. Rather, I suggest ways to increase family-of-God realities in the typical congregation that is known by most readers.

For Whom Is This Book Intended?
This book is written for all those who lead congregations,

by whatever names they are called. They may be called elders, deacons, pastors, church council, official board members, bishops, ministers, priests, presbyters, deaconesses, council members, vestrymen, or some other name.

In discussing the leading of a congregation, I never address pastors alone. I always address the team of which the pastor is a part. While elders and deacons are clearly in mind, they are never seen apart from the pastor.

Any group of concerned youth or adults, who care about helping their congregation to grow in warmth, caring, closeness, belonging, and shared life as members of God's family, will find this book interesting, and helpful.

I suggest that this book be read with an actual congregation in mind. As you read, test each suggestion for its usefulness in your congregation. A group of congregational leaders may find it useful to wrestle and weigh my suggestions in relation to their own congregation.

What This Book Seeks to Accomplish

I will address you personally as congregational leaders. I do not offer a perfect package, or a complete program which any and every congregation should adopt. I know very well that there is great variation among congregations and no one plan or program could fit them all.

Rather in this book I am offering for your consideration twenty suggestions, each one described in a separate chapter, which might help your congregation to move a little closer to being the family of God. Your congregation might find that only three or four will fit your need now. Another congregation may seize upon several other ones in light of their situation. So be it. Whether one or many, the goal of these suggestions is to help your congregation in its own way and situation to move a little nearer to the loving fellowship, the vital life, the tender burden-bearing, and the shared reality which God desires for His sons and daughters in their common life.

After each chapter several books are suggested for those

who wish to peruse further the ideas that have been introduced.

In Appreciation

I am indebted to those congregations with whom I have worked, both as pastor and bishop, for a twenty-five-year period. Also to my classes in pastoral care, and pastoral leadership at the Associated Mennonite Biblical Seminaries who have challenged, corrected, and inspired my vision for a twenty-year period. (These years overlapped in time with my services as bishop.) In addition I have tested these ideas with many groups of pastors, elders, and congregational leaders in numerous retreat, seminar, and workshop settings.

Special mention must be made of the thorough and constructive criticism given by three of my colleagues from the faculty of the Associated Mennonite Biblical Seminaries. Millard C. Lind of the Bible department, Marlin E. Miller of the history-theology department, and David Augsburger of the work of the church department, each critiqued the manuscript from the perspective of their own discipline and personal conviction. Their helpful suggestions resulted in many improvements of the manuscript.

Jean Kelly typed and retyped the manuscript with loving patience and persistence. Paul M. Schrock, book editor of Herald Press, gave valuable feedback along the way.

For the help of these and many more persons I am grateful. Responsibility for the final product and shape of the ideas is mine alone.

Paul M. Miller
Elkhart, Indiana

Leading the
Family of
God

1

Consider the Congregation
A Family

As congregational leaders, you should function like a family because Jesus Christ, the Lord of the church, seriously intended that His followers should do this. Jesus taught that His followers should group themselves into "households." He began this model by organizing the twelve for mutual support.

Furthermore Jesus taught, "My mother, sister, and brother (my family) are those who commit themselves to share my life and walk my way" (Matthew 12:50). He intended that anyone who chooses to be His disciple should discover, in glad surprise, that he or she has fallen heir to "one-hundred-fold brothers, sisters, and mothers." He intended that the new reality of the family of God would make it normal for members to use the intimate term for daddy, "Abba," when they prayed to God. As they so prayed they would feel that the sovereign God to whom they prayed was also the God and Father of their Lord, Jesus Christ, "My Father and your Father, my God and your God." He seriously intended for them to be "firstborn among many brethren." Therefore Christ picked the "family" as the best model for the congregational life of His followers.

He expected that their loyalty to God's family would supersede human family loyalties. In times of apostasy, if need be, His followers would choose to "hate their human father and mother," rather than to deny Christ. Even the supreme expression of human family loyalty, helping to "bury my father," would be left for the spiritually dead to take care of, if divine family loyalties demanded it. Christ's instruction to a leader among His disciples was "when you are converted, strengthen your brethren."

Christ wanted His disciples to be joined in bands of such intense mutual commitment and caring that they would use plural pronouns in their private prayers. Seldom would a disciple pray, "My Father, give me my daily bread, forgive me my debts, deliver me from evil." Rather their group identity would be so strong that each individual would pray, "Our Father . . . give us . . . deliver us . . . forgive us. . . . "

The Apostle John Favored It

The Apostle John intended that the followers of Jesus would band themselves together to form families of God. But because of rapidly moving events He was unable to spell this model out in detail.

John foresaw that the experience of a new birth, a shift in identity, and a commonness and love for one another would form Christ's disciples into a single cohesive unit. He perceived that they would claim kinship with a common Father, and with a common Elder Brother Jesus Christ. He noted that the crucial proof that a person has passed from death into life was precisely "because we love the brethren."

John frequently used household phrases to describe the relationship among the disciples of Christ: "my little children"; "beloved"; "he who loves his brother"; "I write to you, children, because you know the Father"; "you will abide in the Son and in the Father"; "beloved, you are God's children now"; "he who does not love his brother is not of God"; "we ought to lay down our lives for the brethren"; and "he who loves God should love his brother also." These are only a sample of the phrases he employed to stress this reality.

Peter Did Too

Peter also believed that future disciples would be joined into a people, and would relate to one another as members of an extended family. He stressed the realities of a common Father, and of being born anew into God's family.

Peter called the church the "household of God," a reality which reflects the continuing life of a common ancestor, a common tradition, and a common name. Members of the household are God's very own people. In the Old Testament this core reality was reflected through God's dealing with Abraham as a clan, Moses as a royal priesthood, David and Solomon as a holy nation (1 Peter 2:9), and has continued among God's people ever since.

Peter desired that a Christian's experience in the family of God would be so vital that members would seek to carry on the family tradition of holiness, and would make for themselves the claim of being precious and dearly loved. He hoped that Christians would take their stand as God's family, and from that reality relate to the other institutions of society. He hoped that the family reality would sustain them in their sufferings; within it exchange the kiss of love; and because of it dare to believe in their future inheritance and glory.

The Apostle Paul Urged It

The Apostle Paul, great founder of congregations across the world, also believed in the family model for congregational life. By contrast He could have borrowed other models, such as the Jewish synagogue, the tribal village, or the Greek city-state but he chose not to.

Paul believed in the family so deeply that, when he listed the qualifications for congregational leaders, he made their proven abilities as a householder one of their first and most important qualifications. He saw the successful guidance of a human household as preparation for successfully guiding a congregation. Four times in 1 Timothy, chapter 3, verse 5, he insisted upon this transfer of learning. "If a man does not know how to manage his own household, how can he care for God's church?"

When he sent Timothy to Ephesus to lead the church there, he provided instructions—"So ... you may know how one ought to behave in the household of God" (1 Timothy 3:15). He dared to believe that Timothy, as an unmarried pastor, could give family-of-God love and caring, even to a single woman— "Treat ... younger women like sisters, in all purity" (1 Timothy 5:2). Paul was confident that agape love was stronger than erotic love, and that family-of-God love could remain sexually chaste.

Paul intended that the congregational members should regard themselves as an "extended family." "Treat every older man as your father, every older woman as your mother, and every young man as your brother" (1 Timothy 5:1). The congregation was to stand ready to support each human family, ready "to be burdened" with care of a needy widow (1 Timothy 5:16).

Paul urged that the congregation be partial toward one another's failures. As in a good household, they are to discuss money matters frankly and clarify sex roles. He examined the depth of their brother love. "I have heard of your ... love toward all the saints" (Ephesians 1:15). To the congregation at Thessalonia he observed, "And indeed you do love all the brethren."

You Can Urge It and Work for It

Members of your congregation can realize that they are the family of God. They can find in the congregation the ties of love, the realities of belonging that are even richer than what they experience in their human families. Happy are those who find family-of-God realities in both their home and congregation, in their human extended family or clan, and in the church.

In good families, members join their destinies. Once a child, always a child. The relationship never really ends. The sorrow of one is felt by all, and the joys of one are to be shared by all. You will be wise to seek this realization in your congregation.

In good families, members make themselves almost totally

liable for one another, and vulnerable to one another. They leave other loves and loyalties in order to cleave to one another. Central in all households is the free acceptance of a mutual bond. (In chapter 2 I invite you to examine the presence or absence of such covenant love.)

Good families enter commitment and covenant, and not a mere contract. Partners promise to take one another "for better or for worse" and children are welcomed just as they are, brilliant or retarded, disabled or healthy. In contrast to contracts, covenants do not include an escape clause or termination date. New members enter by a baptismal covenant-vow. They promise to give counsel to and receive counsel from the church.

Good families have a prodigal abandon for one another. The son's prodigal failure is met by the Father's prodigal love. Mother's love is uncalculating, ready to sacrifice, and ready to suffer, like God's own love. Within this framework of accepting love, each member can say "we" without losing his or her own individuality. In such a mutual bond of belonging, members can be autonomous individuals.

Family commitments are a public, not a private affair. These commitments provide dependable structures upon which society can rely. Family members, helpless innocents, and the infirm aged can depend upon them for support and structure. In families, as God intended them, members receive what they need and contribute what they can, without financial calculation.

Your goal as leaders of God's family is to provide models in your congregational life which your members can follow in their human families. The way you provide for the widows who have no human families or relatives jogs the conscience of those who are tempted to ignore their obligations. By your example you warn them that those who fail their obligations have denied the faith and are worse than infidels.

You instruct your members that they should be faithful in their human relationships out of reverence for Christ (Ephesians 5:21). You emphasize that servants can perform their humble duties as unto the Lord (Colossians 3:18-25). You teach that marriage partners are to look to Christ's relationship to the church as the model for their marriage relationship. You note that even the believing woman, who is married to a man who refused to enter the family of God, should draw strength from the congregation to live a godly and winsome life within her badly divided human family (1 Peter 3:1).

The deeper meanings of faith, hope, and love are learned in the family of God, and then transferred back to the human family. In both their human and divine families, your members need the modeling of unselfish love, supportive companionship in crises, confessing and forgiving faults, and interacting fellowship in both faith and work. Everyone, in all stages of life, needs the guidance and help of the congregation in meeting and successfully completing his or her developmental tasks.

As leaders of the congregation you call one another brother and sister. No one is doctor, reverend, or boss. All are adult children and Jesus Christ is elder brother. All are heirs and joint heirs with Christ. Both by the analogy of the new birth and by adoption as sons you claim family linkage. You admonish members to live in harmony with one another because you are family.

No other working or gifting of God's Spirit is more cherished than the Holy Spirit's enabling of the cry, "Abba, Father." No other motive for mutual aid is so strong as "do good to all men, but especially to those who are of the household of faith" (Galatians 6:10). You constantly remind members not to seek only their own interests, but also the interest of other members in God's household.

Strangeness which new converts feel at first is to be quickly overcome because they are now members of the household of God (Ephesians 2:19). Believers are just as surely God's family while here on earth as are those who are part of the family of God in heaven. You expect members to yearn for one another with the affection of Christ. Such love is the perfect bond of union.

Tender concerns not to offend another member of the congregation are based upon the fact that he or she is a brother or sister for whom Christ died. Terms of endearment come naturally. The "holy hug" occurs spontaneously at times. Even though there is much giving and receiving, there are no debtors and creditors. Each is to owe no one anything but to love one another.

When in evangelism a convert has been led to faith, the new believer is "my child ... whose father I have become," as Paul said of Onesimus (Philemon 10). Paul calls the mother of Rufus "his mother and mine" (Romans 16:13). The entire church in Rome is to love one another with brotherly affection. Family relationships and love are first of all God's gift, but expressing family love in hundreds of specific ways is a specific act of the will, an affirmation of God's will for His children.

Suggested Readings

For those of you who wish to read further, I suggest an older, but still relevant book by Paul E. Johnson, *Christian Love,* Abingdon Press (O.P.). A second book is Benjamin Zablocki's *The Joyful Community,* University of Chicago Press, revised 1980, paper.

Discussion Suggestions

List the characteristics of "family" which are already operating in your congregation. Then discuss additional emphases or methods you might initiate to increase family reality. How might you get all of your members involved in this discussion and quest?

2

Affirm That You Do Belong to One Another

If you are serious about leading the congregation as God, the King, desires His household of heirs to be led, you can ask members to take their membership seriously. They will need to see themselves as God's children, as settlers from another country, planted here in a strange land. They will need strong determination in order to help one another to live and act as God's faithful children.

God has always expected His people to live within covenant. God's covenant began with the old covenant (Testament) with Israel and climaxed in the new covenant (Testament) through Christ's sacrificial death. God expects you as leaders to insist upon covenants and vows as each new member enters the congregation through baptism. Because of this you may be wise to include the renewal and recommitment of the baptismal vows as a part of the service when new members are received by church letter.

Enter Covenants with One Another

You can urge convenanting because lonely people need ties of genuine belonging. Those who flaunt their solitary freedoms can never know the more profound freedom which waits for those willing to bind themselves to one another in a great cause and a shared life. Some of your members will resist covenanting because they were hurt by legalism in their past, and others because they are not sure enough of their own identity to get close to other people.

Just as persons who desire to merely "shack up" rather than to take upon themselves the vows and covenant of marriage find that they have deceived themselves, in the same way those who desire vital church membership without covenanting also deceive themselves.

There is an oral tradition abroad in your congregation as to the commitment expected of each member. By putting these expectations into writing, you will help to clarify the ways in which the congregation is different from all other groups in society.

Other groups in society invite persons to join their ranks in order to escape from loneliness, to achieve prestige, or to be amused. Still others offer an acceptable outlet for aggression such as certain hate groups. Some groups offer fun, security, challenge, or nostalgia. Other groups offer support, strength, anonymity, and belonging.

But as congregational leaders you can invite your people to respond to your heavenly Father's invitation to His feast of good things. In this covenanting process you invite believers to join because they are already one in spirit. A unity in the shared life of Christ is already there, waiting to be acknowledged. Each individual who has said, "Jesus is Lord," now asks the congregation to hold him or her accountable to really allow Jesus to be Lord in daily decisions.

Persons are invited to join because God's family is waiting to become their truest family. This new family is more than a mere substitute for the human family they left, through psychological weaning, when they became adult. Entrance into God's family is experienced as a quiet miracle of grace.

Persons may join God's family seeking to experience the felt presence of Christ in their midst. Jesus promised them His presence when believers "meet in my name." God's kingdom periodically breaks in with power when children of God pray to their Father, "Let Thy kingdom come."

Persons may join God's family seeking honest interchange, speaking the truth in love. They may be weary of wearing masks and are looking for loving hands to hold the mirror and to tell them how they really appear to other people.

Persons may join God's forgiving community because they believe that if they will walk out into the light of honest interchange, as Christ is in the light, they can know a new kind of fellowship, and the forgiveness of Christ can go on and on cleansing them from sins.

It is useful to state some of these desires, intentions, expectancies, and promises in a covenant. Covenants are promises of love, expressing sincere intentions, making clear what each intends to give and hopes to receive. All legalistic language is to be avoided, for covenants are not rules to keep, but mutual understandings and promises persons have gladly made in complete freedom. In line with this spirit, no penalties for failure are included in the covenant statement.

Promise to Help One Another in Specific Ways

In covenants members usually state their intentions about attendance, their agreement to keep one another's deeply shared experiences in strictest confidence, and their commitment of mutual aid and sharing when a crisis overtakes any one of them. Some groups agree that no "official decisions" will be made if more than two members are unable to be present.

For groups who want to go deeper in their relationship, members agree to share spiritual burdens, sorrows, testings, or crises, and promise to pray for one another as the Spirit prompts. Some groups promise to help one another to discern their Holy Spirit-given gifts for ministry. Others agree to undergird one another in intercessory prayer for the task each one faces in the human family. Some promise mutual aid even to the sharing of savings.

Some agree to practice Matthew 18 quite literally if hurts or misunderstandings occur. In such groups it is best for each member to feel keenly the responsibility to give counsel and to receive counsel from the group. As each member "walks-out-into-the-light" (as Christ is in the light) in truthfulness and honesty, then the forgiving love from God and one another can flow in.

You can expect that your covenant will include promises which some members feel more deeply about than others. Some may want to advocate refusal to pay the portion of taxes that support the national defense and military program, whereas others will merely want to support individual members who feel led to do so. Some may want to initiate ecumenical contacts with other Christians in the area whereas others will want to be open to opportunities which come naturally. Some may want to pledge one percent of their gross income for Third World development whereas others will want to encourage it. Some may want to use strong language against individualism such as "crucifying the ego" whereas others will want to affirm the blending of autonomy and commonality. Thus covenants should stress both individuality and community and both closeness and distance.

Some may want written statements of doctrinal beliefs. Others may want to incorporate specific leadership roles and titles, believing that titles like shepherd, overseer, apostle, enabler, facilitator, and advocate, are important. Some many want to spell out the status of those who wish to participate but are not yet ready to enter the covenant, such as "intentional neighbors," or "friends of the church."

You may well covenant to cooperate with your area or district body of congregations. You may wish to study other covenants which congregations are finding helpful. (You can secure copies by writing to other congregational or district leaders.) But you should never copy a covenant developed by another congregation. To be binding, your members should at least modify it to suit their special circumstances.

A minimal covenant usually includes a statement of personal vow of faithfulness to Jesus Christ and a promise to allow Christ's Spirit to join oneself to a visible body of His followers. Baptismal vows among earlier Mennonite groups included the promise to give counsel and to receive counsel from the church.

Fuller covenants spell out intentions in more detail, such as the members' sincere intention to attend, to be open to admonition, to become part of a face-to-face group in which admonition can realistically happen, and to steward all of one's gifts and resources for Christ's kingdom.

In addition, some groups include their intention to practice nonresistant love in reconciling all relationships. Some include the promise to support one another as each person penetrates society redemptively. Some covenants include agreements regarding mutual decision-making, mutual aid and financial help in crises, mutual discernment of vocational choices, mutual counter-signing of budgets, and mutual transparency and honesty.

Allow Groups to Go as Deep as They Choose

A few groups choose to go all the way to mutual sharing of housing, personal property, and economic destiny. Your congregation may welcome a subgroup like this, but rarely will an entire congregation decide to become a full Bruderhof in the total sharing of their monies.

Persons influenced by fundamentalism will want their covenant to emphasize doctrine, so that everyone will have the same understandings of such doctrines as the virgin birth, the new birth, the plenary-verbal inspiration of the Scriptures, eternal heaven-and-hell, and the Trinity. Those influenced by a believers' church theology will want to covenant to follow Christ's teachings in the Sermon on the Mount as fully as His divine Spirit enables.

As leaders, you will likely find that creedal covenants quickly degenerate into sterile heresy hunting. Covenants to help one another to follow Christ in life are more productive and truer to New Testament models. Thus you will be wise to include both word and deed, both thought and action and both union and separation in your covenant statements.

If your congregation is small, you may assemble a covenant which grows out of what your members are already laying-on-the-line for the congregation. How much priority do congregational meetings have in agendas and date books? How much commitment is there to tithe or to give beyond the tithe? A record of these intrinsic commitments which are already guiding the lives of your members can be the beginning of your congregational covenant.

If your congregation is large, the covenant should be limited to a few basic promises. Then you can encourage the smaller face-to-face groups such as clusters, house fellowships, prayer groups, or Sunday school classes to be more detailed in their covenanting.

Provide a Time for Renewing of Covenants

You will be wise also to periodically provide time for the renewal of covenants. History warns us that the most living covenant can become unmeant, dead, and a vestige of legalism. A covenant renewal service may be held during a watch-nite service at New Year's time, at the annual members' meeting, or when new members are asked to come under the covenant and make their vows as they receive water baptism.

In covenant making, remember that you will always have some reluctant ones. Individualism is so rampant, and proud self-centeredness is so pervasive that covenanting will never become easy. You may need to provide a friends-of-the-church category for those who wish to attend and to participate as they are willing and able, but who cannot yet see their way clear to enter into a meaningful covenant. Thus it is important that all covenants recognize the free will and choice of each believer, as well as group loyalty and belonging.

One Kind of Covenant Renewal Service

In order to renew and deepen the sense of covenant with

God and His people, you may decide to lead the congregation in a liturgical covenant renewal service several times a year. Following is a portion of a covenant renewal service used by the Church of South India:*

Prayer Led by the Minister

O God, who hast appointed our Lord Jesus Christ as Mediator of a new covenant, grant us grace we beseech thee to draw near with fullness of faith and join ourselves in a perpetual covenant to thee; through the same Jesus Christ our Lord.

**Amen.

Scripture Lessons (congregation standing)

Old Testament:	Jeremiah 31:31-33
Epistle:	Hebrews 12:22-25a
Gospel:	Matthew 11:27-30 (congregation seated)

The Covenant Call

And now, beloved, let us with all our heart renew our part in the covenant that God has made with his people, and take the yoke of Christ upon us. This taking of his yoke means that we are heartily content that he should appoint us our place and work, and that he alone should be our reward.

Christ has many services to be done; some are easy, others are difficult; some bring honour, others bring reproach; some are suitable to our natural inclinations and temporal interests, others are contrary to both. In some we may please Christ and please ourselves, in others we cannot please Christ except by denying ourselves. Yet the power to do all these things is assuredly given us in Christ, who strengtheneth us.

Therefore let us make the covenant of God our own. Let us engage our heart to the Lord, and resolve in his strength never to go back.

Being thus prepared, let us now, in sincere dependence on his grace and trusting in his promises, yield ourselves anew to him, meekly kneeling upon our knees.

---

*The Book of Common Worship, Oxford University Press, 1964, pp.136 and 137.

**Congregation reads in unison.

The Prayer

O Lord God, Holy Father, who hast called us through Christ to be partakers in this gracious covenant, we take upon ourselves with joy the yoke of obedience, and engage ourselves, for love of thee, to seek and do thy perfect will. We are no longer our own, but thine.

The Covenant Response by the Congregation

**I am no longer my own, but thine. Put me to what thou wilt, rank me with whom thou wilt; put me to doing, put me to suffering; let me be employed for thee or laid aside for thee, exalted for thee or brought low for thee; let me be full, let me be empty; let me have all things, let me have nothing; I freely and heartily yield all things to thy pleasure and disposal.

Intentions

On the basis of these affirmations I covenant to participate faithfully in the worship, nurture, fellowship, and decision-making occasions of the congregation, and to become, involved in a small class or group in which I can experience mutual counsel, forgiveness, nurture, and support for those personal disciplines essential for growth in Christ.

I covenant to hold in trust all the material, personal, and spiritual resources which God commits to me, and to accept the counsel of my brothers and sisters in lifestyle and giving, seeking to keep my use of material goods and services under the constraint of the cross.

I covenant to seek to live by Christ's example of forgiving, accepting, nonresistant, nondiscriminating love as his way to minister reconciliation in a world torn by alienation and violence.

I covenant to help identify new issues as they confront the church in its prophetic witness and sharing the good news in deed and word in daily relationships.

I covenant to review with my fellow believers the faithfulness of my Christian walk as a means of supporting spiritual integrity and usefulness, and to consider membership in a local fellowship so important that when I move from this community I will seek out a congregation in which to nurture my obedience to Christ.

Together we confess our need of God's forgiveness and daily strengthening. May the God whom we know through his revelation in Christ and the church be praised by our lives.

**And now, O Glorious and blessed God, Father, Son, and Holy Spirit, thou art mine, and I am thine. So be it. And the covenant which I have made on earth, let it be ratified in heaven. Amen. (Silent meditation)

Even a Larger Congregation Can Affirm Its Intentions

A Proposed Covenant Statement

We, the _____ Church are a voluntary community of faith in God, who affirm His authority as revealed in the old and new covenants and supremely in His Son, Jesus Christ. We are debtors to the whole Christian tradition, but support and are shaped more directly by the Anabaptist heritage. By the power of the Holy Spirit we seek to follow Christ in partnership with other congregations of common purpose throughout the world. We offer these expressions of our faith and intention as our understandings for church membership. We anticipate growth in knowledge and response as we help each other discern the mind of Christ.

Affirmations

As a member I affirm that God is always at work calling and forming His people. He sent His Son to live as a suffering servant, to offer Himself as my Savior, and to rise and reign forever as Lord. Because I believe Jesus is Lord, God is making me one of His people.

I affirm that Christ unites us by His Spirit in His body, in which we are members interdependent, mutually supportive and mutually accountable. In the midst of the struggle of God's kingdom against the evil one, the Holy Spirit creates in us spiritual worship, trusting relationships, faithful discipleship, and effective witness.

A House Fellowship Can Create a More Intimate Covenant

Recognizing the need for a small-group expression of the church in each of our lives, we covenant together. Our group will work within the structures of the _____ congregation. Each member will maintain a vital relationship with the local congregation.

Covenant of Group Members

1. I will prepare for our agreed agenda, and will attend our meetings each week, on time.

2. I will pray in response to the promptings of the Spirit for our meetings and for group members.

3. I will participate in the group life with caring love by sharing honestly, listening attentively, supporting, confronting, counseling, confessing, and forgiving.

4. I will faithfully keep confidences shared in the group.

5. I will share in mutual discernment of gifts within our group, and will make my gifts available to the group.

6. I will be generous in sharing possessions, time, energy, and other resources at my disposal, when they are needed by other members of the group.

7. I will commit my life to service for Christ, His church, and His world, with the support of the group. I will support the other members of the group in their avenues of service in the world.

8. I will discuss with the group any major exceptions to the intent of this covenant, or any need to withdraw from the group.

9. I will share periodically in an evaluation of the group's covenant and life together.

Suggested Readings

For parallel readings you may want to read Dave and Neta Jackson's *Living Together in a World Falling Apart,* Creation House, 1974, paper; and Paul M. Miller's *Peer Counseling in the Church,* Herald Press, 1978.

Discussion Suggestions

In a congregational meeting, discuss what additional milestones (in addition to baptisms, marriages, and funerals) your members would like either to celebrate or solemnize together. What are the next steps to get such sharing going in your congregation?

3

Recognize Each Member's Unique Gifts

As leaders of God's household you believe that God brings each person's unique gift into the group and blends it marvelously and miraculously with all others. The group thus becomes a functioning whole, a body, a family, in which every member is important.

You will be wise to reread the scriptural passages on "spiritual gifts," and keep asking yourselves what this means for the way you discern and call forward gifted leaders. You may want to have your preacher-teacher-equipper to expound Romans 12:4-8, 1 Corinthians 12:4-10, Ephesians 4:8-12, and 1 Peter 4:10, 11, and discuss in your adult and youth classes or intergenerational clusters how these truths apply in your congregation.

God's Gifts Are for His Whole Family

The ascended Christ intends to run His church by sending gifts to "gift coveters" within your congregation (Ephesians 4:8). If your congregation seems cold and unfriendly, instead of griping about the fact (which only makes it worse) your gift-coveting members should ask the ascended Christ to give the charismatic gift of hospitality to some of your members. You should covet earnestly the gift of prophesy and ecstasy so that reality and joy will liven up your gatherings. If your congregation is floundering for understanding, covet gifts of wisdom and knowledge; if it is stalled in program, covet the gifts of administration; if timid members need support, covet the gift of "helps"; and if convictions on ethical issues are fuzzy, covet the gift of teaching. The ascended Christ gives these gifts to specific members of your congregation. It is your challenge to discern to whom He has given specific gifts and to find a way to call these gifted persons into service.

Gifted Members Begin Serving One Another in Love

Persons who are being gifted by the Holy Spirit and enabled to edify the congregation should first of all begin to volunteer and to serve with their gifts in the many ways which are constantly open to them. Members energized by love and by Spirit gifts can begin to bind broken hearts, to speak words of deliverance to persons who seem to be captive, help the blinded persons to see, and announce God's jubilee, his setting free. They can do as Jesus did when He was gifted beyond measure by the Holy Spirit—He just went about doing good. He fed and taught the poor, loved the children, talked to the rich, taught about His Father, helped people find forgiveness, and urged the repentant ones to begin again. Demonstration is the first and supreme way for spiritual gifts to become noticed. Those who are truly gifted by God's Spirit do not need an office or a title in order to begin their ministry.

Gifts Are Seen During Sharing Times in the Church

Gifts can also show themselves during the "concerns of the church" period, an informal, sharing time in the weekly corporate worship service. Here gifts of prophecy can be used to admonish the congregation, gifts of tongues can lead out in exulting worship, gifts of teaching can clarify a truth, and gifts of knowledge can offer "common sense" about a current issue. Often this sharing period will remind you of the gifted congregation in Corinth. Paul said, in 1 Corinthians 14:26, "When you come together, each one has a hymn, a lesson, a revelation, a tongue, or an interpretation. Let all things be done for edification."

A Gift-Discernment Committee Can Serve You

As leaders of God's gifted children, you will be well advised to have the congregation select a "gift-discernment committee" whose responsibility it is to tap-on-the-shoulder persons whom God's Spirit is obviously gifting. Some should be called forward and assigned an office or task in the congregation which will evoke and utilize their gift to the full. However, not every gifted member needs to be given an official task, but all should be encouraged to exercise their gifts freely and fully in voluntary ways.

Your gift-discernment committee may lead the congregation to utilize the face-to-face groups of the church (such as clusters, house fellowships, adult Sunday school classes, prayer groups, etc.) to carry out the gift-discernment process. With a list of the church offices, committees, commissions, and servants before them, members of a face-to-face group can seek to discern who in their group is being given the gift needed for a given position in the church. This process may continue in free and prayerful discussion until every member of the group has been challenged to ponder whether God's Spirit is indeed gifting and calling him or her to a given service. The results of this small group process can be brought together by the gift-discernment committee and reported back to the congregation.

Small Groups Can Do Gift Discernment

Some small groups may find it useful to begin the gift-discernment process by dividing into groups of two who know each other rather well. Each person then is invited to tell his or her dyad partner three things. First, "what I have done in Christian service which I feel best utilized my God-given gifts"; second, "what I hope I can do sometime in the future in Christian service"; and third, "which gifts I hope to utilize in and through our gathered life as a congregation, and which ones I hope to utilize through my scattered life in my daily work."

After the couple has shared intimately around these three questions, the dyad partners return to the full group and each person tells the group what he or she heard the partner say. The group members then continue the discussion, suggesting which task in the church they feel each one is gifted to do.

Whatever method is used, you will be wise to lead your congregation beyond the dreary democratic voting process to fill church offices. Your members are tired having to vote "no" against one another on a typical ballot. They are not convinced that the majority vote is the best way to discern God's gifted prophet or servant in their midst. They can't agree that the one who received 51 percent of the votes was fully called of God, and the one who got 49 percent wasn't called at all.

Apparently the ascended Christ gives gifts for a specific ministry at a given point in time. Thus you need not hurry to assign an office to every member in line with a ministry-gift the person possesses. It may be that God's Spirit comes upon the person for a given ministry only at intermittent times. When the congregation needs to be edified, then God's Spirit may gift a member to help, teach, prophesy, give, heal, administer, or interpret. These God-given gifts do not seem to be a permanent possession of an individual like are blue eyes, high IQ, height, or talents. However, some members are given the same gift for long periods of time.

Gifts Enrich Gathered and Scattered Life....

You will be wise to regard charismatic gifts as the group's property given to help the congregation to function together as God's family. No member should claim a gift and affix it to his or her name as one would an earned academic degree. Gifts are given by Christ to enable God's family to continue to do those ministries of love which Jesus began to do when He was bodily present in the world.

Although charismatic gifts seem to be given primarily to

enrich the group's life when they are gathered, the strengthening may linger on to bless the lives of members during their scattered life of service in the world. Thus the person gifted with faith during the church meeting may be stronger all week while on the job, the person gifted with knowledge may be wiser for issues faced in his or her weekly work, and the person gifted to help others in church may be a better helper all week.

A Few Cautions About Gift Discernment

A few cautions are in order. You will be wisest to limit your gift discernment for actual needs and tasks. Gifts are given to edify the church for actual needs and tasks, for fulfilling her mission. You are well advised to discourage gift discernment unrelated to real service for Christ and the church. Such gift-discernment sessions can easily sag into mutual flattery occasions. Members end up giving each other vague psychological compliments. It is not very useful for kingdom service for church members to sit around telling each other things like—"I discern that you have artistic creativity," or "I discern that you have contagious optimism," or "I discern that you have a warm spirit or a beautiful smile," or "I discern that you have the gift of teaching." God-given gifts are never given for private enjoyment or pride, but always to edify the congregation for its mission.

You should be aware that the gift-discernment process can become so long-drawn-out and laborious that members come to dread it, and to resist going through it again. You will be wise to keep this pitfall in mind as you plan the way your congregation will work at this.

You may experience another undesirable outcome if you allow persons to bring pressure upon one another to accept assignments in order to utilize the gifts which have been discerned. Under the loving encouragement of the members of their group, some persons may promise more than they should, and may undertake more service assignments than their total life schedule may allow. As a result great frustration and discouraged resignation may come to some, while compulsive overwork and busyness which is destructive to family life may come to others.

Suggested Readings

Books for further study of gift discernment and enlistment may include Gordon Cosby's *Handbook for Mission Groups,* Word Books (O.P.); Donald Bridge and David Phyper's book, *Spiritual Gifts and the Church,* Inter-Varsity Press, 1973, paper; Wolfgang Roth and Rosemary R. Reuther's *The Liberating Bond,* Friendship Press, 1978; and C. Peter Wagner's book *Your Spiritual Gifts Can Help Your Church Grow,* Regal Books, 1980.

Discussion Suggestions

Reexamine the promises (or covenant) new members are making as they join your congregation by baptism, by church letter, and by confession of faith. Discuss as leaders what you would want to add to these promises to have it become your congregational covenant. How would your members respond if you invited them publicly, as a group, to renew their covenants with God and with one another just after new members declare their covenants (or vows) to become members? How else might you establish covenanting and renewing of covenants in your congregation?

4

Expect All Members to Be Volunteers

In the famly of God you can honor both the individual and the group. Therefore you honor the inner calls which members sense as well as encourage them to volunteer for ministry in the congregation.

A commune may teach its members that rugged individualism is terribly wrong, and only collectivism is right, but in the congregation you honor each individual as well as the group. In leading the household of God, you need to hear what God is saying through every member of His family. All of God's children are equally important, even the most feeble are necessary, and the most childlike are pioneers in His kingdom.

You will assemble your congregational goals partly from what God is saying to each member. Light for your congregation's way will clarify as each one brings his or her "candle" of insight and wisdom.

Invite Members to Volunteer Their Ideas and Concerns

How shall individual calls and convictions be brought together? You can make the "concerns-of-the-church" time during the corporate worship service as an invitation to every member to speak out, to share concerns, calls, convictions, and leadings which God's Spirit is laying on his or her heart.

You can establish an "opinion board" in the foyer of your church. Here members are invited to post "proposals," concerns for a project in mission, or suggestions for congregational action. It is important that a proposal be reasonable, clearly outlined, at least partially reachable, courageous and challenging, complete with budget implications, and with some next steps suggested toward its realization. (See Appendix A "Brief Form for Writing a Proposal" for a suggested format of a proposal.)

Members who agree and want to volunteer to help a given proposal to "get-off-the-ground" can sign their names beneath the name of the originator of the proposal. When 6 or 10 names have been added, involving at least 4 or 5 families of the congregation, then the proposal can be lifted from the "opinion board" and brought into a duly called congregational meeting for official action.

Provide an Empty Chair in Your Leaders' Meetings

In addition to invitations during "concerns-of-the-church" sharing period, and invitations to post proposals on the opinion board, your leadership team, elders, or governing board can let it be known that an "empty chair" will be maintained in every meeting for any member to come and claim when he or she wants to share a conviction or proposal. In God's family it is important that you make it easy and natural for every member to be heard.

You can invite members to bring to the church meeting concerns which grow upon them in the midst of their daily work. Members penetrate many arteries of society all week when they are the church scattered. They may need the help of fellow Christians to discover additional ways to be a Christian presence in their daily work.

Encourage Volunteering in the Community

As God's household in your community you may want to support or back some of the helping agencies which persons of good will are operating. Because you appreciate what is being done for the blind, the deaf, the retarded, the crippled, or the helpless, you may ask such agencies to allow your congregation to appoint a liaison to their agency. This liaison representative might attend their board meetings as an observer and bring back to your congregation prayer concerns and suggestions of specific ways your congregation can help. Many of such agencies need an infusion of Christ's Spirit of caring to keep their difficult tasks up to the most helpful level.

Be Aware of Problems Which Go Along with Volunteering

You as leaders need to be realistically aware that, whereas the church relies very heavily upon the volunteer spirit for her work, and uses volunteering persons to lead out in much that she does, yet there are problems with a heavy use of the volunteering method. It is true that volunteers are usually highly motivated and are ready for much sacrificial service beyond the line of duty. Yet some volunteers are misfits, power hungry, and not the kind of persons the group would have selected.

You will be wise leaders if you always keep the call for volunteers balanced by the test of group approval and appointment. Keep teaching constantly that God's inner call to the individual must be tested and always corroborated by the group's call before a worker is officially approved to lead out in an area of work.

Beware If Pay Becomes the Main Motive

Be careful not to let the false notion emerge that volunteers serve free, and that elected staff are always paid. Even ordained workers need not always be paid, but should serve freely, as volunteers, if financially able to do so. Some retired persons will want to donate large amounts of time freely, and the gift of their time should be welcomed.

In the secular world the ability to command high pay for one's time is a big part of a person's self-confidence. Assertiveness training teaches persons to show how much they know they are worth by insisting upon liberal pay for what they do. God's prophets and apostles always protested this spirit. The most sensitive and understanding therapists warn that such a marketing orientation toward oneself is detrimental to true self-respect. Imagine Amos, Jeremiah, Jesus, and Paul linking their self-respect to the size of their salary!

Rather you will arrange to pay anyone whose real need calls for pay, and accept free service from any whose need is not such that pay is important. Usually when someone's church work impinges upon the 40 hours per week which most persons need to make a living, then you should check to see whether pay is needed from the church.

Volunteers Do Have Special Needs

As leaders you should be aware that volunteer workers need and appreciate some special considerations, which may not be as important for paid staff. They need careful orientation for their part-time work. They need flexible scheduling to fit their free time. They need to feel that their gifts match the tasks they are asked to do. They need to sense that their volunteer efforts are coordinated well with the efforts of other volunteers. They need frank suggestions for improvement and expressions of appreciation for what they do well. If they are already donating their time, you should be sure that their incidental costs of mileage, materials, postage, and so forth are paid by the church unless it is clear that they wish to donate these costs too.

When you as leaders rely heavily upon volunteer workers, you should be aware that you need great flexibility, tactful frankness, a keen sense of humor, the ability to give clear instructions, plus the tactful courage to offset power hungers as they arise. No naive reliance upon piety dare blind you to the dynamics which accompany the using of volunteer workers.

Suggested Readings

Further helpful readings concerning the tactful use of volunteers can be found in Eva Schindler-Rainman and Ronald

Lippitt's book *The Volunteer Community: Creative Uses of Human Resources,* 2nd ed., University Associates, 1977, paper, and Kenneth Chafin's book, *Help, I'm a Layman,* Word Books, 1966, paper.

Discussion Suggestions

Discuss how you can continue to encourage volunteering and yet balance this with the wisdom and safety of group discernment. How can you blend "choice by the group" with volunteering by the individual?

5

Remember the Milestones

Becoming God's household, and living together as His family, is both a gift and a task. As leaders, you can rely upon the fact that God's Spirit gives the spirit of sonship as a gift. God's life within members draws them together. God's Word teaches them to live, to share, and to care for each other. God is even now at work to create community in your congregation. God wants to be Father to your congregation as His family, His people, His household. He gives unity as a gift.

Helping Him to do this is your task. You need to provide the rituals, schedules, and the incentives for family life and love to grow and thrive. You can constantly encourage members to "rejoice with them that rejoice, and weep with them that weep." You structure the congregation's life together so that family of God realities will grow.

So, make glad occasions of member's birthdays and special days. Encourage surprise gifts for one another. Provide occasions when members can share what the year of life just passed has taught them about God's love and leading. Celebrate or solemnize many important milestones of member's lives.

Rely upon the artistic skills within your members for these celebrations. Avoid paid entertainers, canned sentiments, or sterile greeting cards, and all that is plastic and superficial. You might have a group enact a skit, "This Is Your Life," portraying the life pilgrimage of the member.

Some wise congregational leaders have developed a "mural for the month," on 4 × 8-foot plywood sheet upon which families place a symbol of God's leading in their family for that month. Families use their combined artistic skill to prepare a symbol of about one foot in diameter, which portrays their feelings about an important event. These may include a birth of a child, a death, a graduation, a housewarming, a tragedy or loss, a promotion, or an anniversary, and so forth. These murals accumulate as the year progresses, around the walls of the church, and help to symbolize God's leading of His pilgrim people that year.

Celebrate Engagements

As leaders you may wish to help the congregation to celebrate and solemnize the day when a member makes an announcement of engagement to be married. Invite the member to share with the congregation how he or she has felt led to covenant together with the chosen partner. If both engaged parties are members of the congregation, suggest that they give their testimonies together and ask for the congregation's prayers. Members can begin to prepare homemade gifts, and in many ways show their loving concern and share in the joy.

If your congregation has reached the necessary level of trust and openness in the giving and receiving of admonition, you may encourage mature members to share with the newly engaged youth what life has taught them about growing deeper into love within marriage. How can each partner be faithful to his or her own unique, developing potential throughout life, and yet not grow apart from one's partner? How can autonomy and freedom be preserved while achieving the deep mutuality and interdependence which is necessary in marriage? How can the partner be set free to grow and to change in faithfulness to his or her own inner call?

Your congregation might encourage its musically gifted members to write a special song, just for this couple. Members who feel called to a ministry of intercessory prayer might carry the engaged couple in prayer that they may live in holiness, purity, and in openness to divine leading. After all, the frightening number of divorces and failings of well-intentioned marriages suggest that couples should seek to discover any fundamental incompatibility before marriage, and respectfully dissolve their engagement. Congregations should reverence the deep, prayerful search which engaged couples are doing to be absolutely sure that they really have lifelong compatibility. Wise young persons may ask advice from their house fellowship.

Make Marriage an Act of Congregational Worship

You will be wise, as congregational leaders, to make the marriage of one of your members a sacred and meaningful occasion. The church has been failing in this area too long and needs renewal. The Apostle Paul insisted that the love of Christ for His bride the church should be the model for human marriages among persons whose lives are centered on Christ. As congregational leaders you will need to work hard, teach steadily, and plan carefully if you are going to have weddings in your congregation that truly embody New Testament ideals. The worldly models are constantly placarded in newspaper accounts, and our drift into worldly patterns is easy. In some congregations these semi-Christian patterns are deeply entrenched already. In your first efforts you can expect some brides and their fond mothers to oppose you.

In contrast to the world's model, which assumes that romantic love has operated, weddings of persons "in Christ" will assume that God has led in answer to trusting prayer. The wedding rite is supremely an act of worship.

Worldly models assume that two individualists made solitary decisions, but churchly weddings will reflect the influence of families and congregations who have given counsel. As part of the wedding celebrations the families of each partner may present skits portraying the growth and lived experience of their son or daughter.

While newspaper accounts of weddings will stress the clothes which the bride and her attendants wore, churchly weddings will accent the vows, the covenants the two partners have agreed upon. Ordinary weddings will include vows from a book, read in perfunctory fashion, not deeply premeditated and meant. But a churchly wedding will have vows written out personally by the bride and groom, with every word weighted, deeply meant, and behind which stands the integrity of the person.

Popular weddings quietly assume that the marriage will endure as long as the partners' romantic attachment shall last. A churchly wedding will assume that the covenants made in life-and-death earnestness, with the intercessory prayers of the church focused upon the partners, will endure as long as life shall last.

Weddings patterned after those in the surrounding culture will appear like a theatrical production, to which visitors come and act like an audience, uninvolved except as a spectator. Churchly weddings will be congregational acts of worship, with everyone actively sharing in the songs, prayers, testimonies, words of exhortation, and renewal of vows and covenants.

Congregations will do well to provide the love feast, the hospitality, the housing for guests, and the loving support of the newlyweds. In earlier eras, bride capture set the families against one another, in bride-price marriages of the third world the clans are in a bargain contract with one another, but in a Christian worship-marriage service, covenants of voluntary love are formed and deepened.

Celebrate High School Graduations

High school graduation is one of the few puberty-rituals or rites of passage which American culture has developed, but the rituals which surround it lack depth of meaning. The graduate usually is within a "happy crisis" about vocational choice, service in the church, and thoughts about a life partner. The graduate is busy clarifying a world-view, a sense of life's meaning, and a discernment of his or her gifts. Society assumes that the graduate is now ready to get a job, get married, go to the army, take up duties as a citizen, and generally settle down.

Your congregation will need wisdom to celebrate a member's graduation in a way fitting to God's family. In God's family those with very little education dare not feel left out. Those who have completed some education must be helped to accept it as God's gift which they need to steward for others.

Your congregation, as God's family, should know many hymns and songs from memory so that in a celebration of a graduation someone may be led by God's Spirit to just that song which captures the deeper meanings and suitably celebrates the occasion.

Your model for a young graduate might well be the public statement which the young man Jesus made to His fellow Jews in His home synagogue in Nazareth. "The Spirit of the Lord is upon me, because he has anointed me to preach good news to the poor. He has sent me to proclaim release to the captives and recovering of sight to the blind, to set at liberty those who are oppressed, to proclaim the acceptable year of the Lord" (Luke 4:18-19).

Celebrate Vocational Choice, Change, or Retirement

You will be wise to help your congregation develop ways to give loving attention to those important milestones. If a member is deciding how to open his or her "sealed orders," how to invest his or her gifts and days, how to serve God and man through a given job or vocation—this should become a "burning bush" where God's personal presence and call are experienced anew. You who lead God's household can encourage suitable rituals to grow regarding these matters.

Persons making vocational choices should be encouraged to share their decisions during "concerns of the church" period and to ask for prayers. Peer counseling should be encouraged, as experienced members make their wisdom available.

Persons who are retiring need more within God's household than they get from secular society. There they get the gold watch, the stilted banquet with its flattery, and the gentle relegation to the "has-beens" of society. God's household may want to find ways to honor the "elders," to invite them to develop a creative hobby, to show that their life's wisdom is truly sought and appreciated, and to open new channels of voluntary service for them through the congregation.

Members who have been fired, laid off, or who are suffering through unemployment and welfare handouts certainly need the loving attention of God's entire household. The Mutual Aid Commission of the congregation should explore their needs in confidential discussions. To each one the congregation needs to know how to give love, caring, emotional support, and assistance which is not demeaning.

Help Parents to Worship When a Child Is Born

As the family of God you will want to think carefully about the sacred event when the creating God gives a child made in His image to one of your human families. Churches which practice infant baptism know how they celebrate the event. But those who believe in adult believer's baptism, and who insist that every infant is safe within the atonement brought by God's Son, seem to have trouble knowing how to celebrate their faith about the child's place in God's family.

Recognize the Deep Gratitude Sincere Parents Feel

You will be wise to recognize the deep and reverent feelings which many sincere parents have as they receive a child from the hands of the creating God. They rely upon Christ's atonement and dare to believe that their child is not a sinner and needs no sacrament to save it. They believe that Christ wants little children to come to Him. They believe that a child's humility, teachableness, sense of awe and wonder, and readiness to forgive should never be lost in the process of becoming adult. In the simple services of worship for use in the home, the cluster of house fellowship, or the congregation, be sure to include statements of thanksgiving, adoration, and praise.

Recognize the Anxieties Parents Struggle to Conceal

Most parents feel like crying out to God in the words of Manoah in Judges 13:8, "Teach us what we are to do with the boy." They recognize the vast potential for good or ill which lies in every person made in God's image. They know how formative and almost normative their own family atmosphere, world-view, assumptions, and example will be. They silently hope the extended family—the congregation—will rally around them and support them as parents and the many relationships of caring, trust, and example their growing child will need. In services of worship, help these feelings to be verbalized.

Recognize the New Commitments Parents Want to Make

There is an awesome finality to becoming a parent. Once a parent always a parent. Self-image is reset. Although marriages can be broken, parenthood cannot. Parents often drop out of many things, form new friendships, rearrange their daily schedules, restructure their budgets. It seems as though the hopes and fears of all of the years meet in the newborn child. Devout parents deeply desire help from you to express these deep feelings. The entire congregation promises to assist in rearing the child by providing loving care, wise counsel, and holy example.

Help Parents of a Retarded or Disabled Child to Cope

If a newborn child is severely retarded or malformed this will be apparent at once. The shock, the anguish, the anger, and the pain of parents is almost beyond description. The dashing of hopes, the despair about giving adequate parental care, and the feeling of being alone is almost more than parents can bear.

These are days and months for the family of God to close ranks around anguished parents in honest, deep, continuing care. A silent and suffering presence is often very helpful. Not many of the most devout and well-informed Christians know how to explain why an all-good creating God who is also all-powerful and could prevent the suffering of innocents, why He allows some innocents to suffer. Not many know what to say when parents cry, "But why me, why us?" Sometimes the anguished cries from Job, the psalmist, or Christ in Gethsemane provide a worship experience of soul-healing depth for these families.

Stand by When Disability Is Discovered Gradually

Parents usually instinctively hope that their children will out-live them, and that through their children they can transcend their own finitude and their approaching death. But when they are slowly forced to admit that their child will not develop normally, may never be able to read or to marry, then their hopes come crashing down in a slow and aweful collapse. Parents often struggle with fears about their own blame, their own "tainted blood," or their own failures. They struggle to avoid either rejecting or overprotecting their retarded or disabled child. Fantasies of sudden cures tend to persist. They debate committing their child to an institution.

Your pastoral care will be listening deeply to their anguish, affirming your caring and the caring of the church, helping sometimes to bear some of the burden and helping them to get away for awhile, and discussing with them the problems of value and faith which nearly always emerge. The constant stress may cause strain in their marriage and may call for intervention by an insightful counselor.

Discuss with them their experiences with needed but difficult discipline of the child. Accept their angers against inconsiderate friends who hint that they are wasting their time. Ask them in what specific ways they wish that the love of God's family would be expressed. Pray with them. Sing with them any songs which meet this need.

Solemnize Sickness, Suffering, with Prayers for Healing

If the congregation is really God's family, members who are experiencing serious illness will get more attention than an announcement in the bulletin, a visit from the pastor and immediate human-family members, and a few canned sentiment get-well cards. Congregational leaders will need to provide ways, both to encourage caring and to channel its expression.

If the stricken member is well enough to be in the meeting, the persons seated nearby may lay-on-hands while spontaneous prayers for healing are poured out. Leaders may be wise to encourage this during "concerns of the church" period in the regular worship service. Some congregations may want to conduct an "anointing with oil and prayers for the sick" service as part of the corporate worship. The anointing oil may be kept on the communion table, in front of the pulpit, along with the open Bible, as one more symbol of a means of grace God has given to his people.

Leaders should quietly teach the right of members to call for the elders of the church to come to their bedside in the home or hospital and conduct the sacred ordinance of anointing with oil according to James 5.

The fullest and richest holistic healing can be symbolized if Christian medical doctors of the congregation are invited to be present and to share in these prayers-for-healing services. This helps to make vivid and real the belief that doctors are also God's agents of healing, and that all healing is God's whether assisted by prayer and/or by medicine.

Members of God's household need to feel free to claim the best that God has given through creation, symbolized by the oil and medicines. In addition God's children can claim the best God has given through the resurrection and the new creation, symbolized by the effectual, fervent prayers of God's people. They "avail much."

You, as leaders, need to be careful that you do not guarantee healing, or feel that you can develop so much faith that God is compelled to heal when you ask Him to. Just because God has healed and honored your prayers of faith so many times, and you know beyond any shadow of doubt that He can heal now if it is His will, beware that you do not presume to always discern His will perfectly. Beware that you do not begin to say that God must always heal, because healing for every sickness is automatically included in Christ's atonement, or because you are a proven healer. If you follow this route, you and your congregation will soon be lost in fanaticism and confusion.

In leading a congregational ministry to such members, be careful not to deify finite well-being or to absolutize perfect health. Allow God to lead you through suffering too, so he can use it redemptively. If God's firstborn Son learned a deeper kind of obedience through suffering, don't be surprised if the part of His family you lead is called to experience periods of suffering too. Nevertheless, do keep praying for healing, in childlike faith, and accept healing when God chooses to give it.

Weep with Those Who Weep

As congregational leaders your best long-range approach will be to get your members started writing living wills which outline the member's own instructions about any heroic measures they either wish or do not wish to be taken on their behalf during terminal illness. As leaders you can model this by writing living wills yourselves, by having tactful and sensitive persons share their living wills with the congregation. At least you can ask all members to deposit in the church office their instructions about the way they wish their home going to be celebrated and solemnized. This will save you a lot of headache and heartache when the crisis of death actually comes.

If you grasp that the congregation is truly God's household, that at death the Father has called a member home to His larger family in heaven, then your rituals and worship services at times of death will be very different from those in the secular and prestige-oriented world around you. You will avoid displays of wealth, insincere flatteries, denials of the reality of death, sub-Christian sentiments in songs or sermon, and phony euphemisms. Canned music, semi-pagan rituals, expensive coffins, and too-lavish floral displays will give way to simple services, simple burials, and rituals which really express Christian faith.

You can encourage and help the congregation to develop ceremonies which point toward fully Christian attitudes toward death. Your rituals can include the Christian attitude toward God's sovereign and wise-loving arbitrariness in allowing some to live on, and allowing some to die. Your services of worship can include sincere Christian testimonies of appreciation for the life-service of the departed. Your services can portray "into thy hands I commend my spirit" as the grandest prayer and the most sublime act of worship a believer can ever offer to God. Your rituals should show how the congregation closes ranks to pick up unfinished tasks of the departed, and assists close family members in doing their ongoing "grief work" in honesty. Your rituals can show how the incident of death is related to the resurrection and the power of an endless life within which all believers may live their remaining days on earth. Your comments may suggest how the many little "deaths to self," which a sincere Christian undergoes, are related to the final death to self which precedes gaining the glorified body and membership in the church triumphant.

The members of your congregation will be a richer family of God if they have developed many songs which solemnize life's darker hours, and if they are prepared to sing their "songs in the night" when a member goes home to God.

In the cases of especially traumatic deaths in your congregation, for which the work of grieving has been unusually difficult and prolonged, you may be wise to plan a service of memory one year after the loved one's death. Grieving relatives sometimes need the congregation's help in remembering their departed dead in a wholesome way. This can be faith-building and therapeutic for them.

One group of congregational leaders planned a memorial service for a Sunday evening in the summer in which congregational members took leisurely walks through the nearby cemetery. Elders and relatives stopped near first one and then another tombstone and retold stories of that particular person's life and ministry. This can help a people keep in touch with their roots.

Expect God's Blessing in the Ordinary Interactions Too

If you model your leadership after that of the Master, you too will try to see meaning in lost sheep, in women baking bread and men building houses, in merchants trading, in sons and daughters rebelling, and in rains descending. You will, like Jesus did, relate every human event to the will of God.

Christ pictured a life together of simple and almost child-like sharing of joys and sorrows. Members rejoice together over the finding of a lost coin, and provide time to take children up into their arms for blessing and benediction. They stop to notice the lilies of the field and birds of the air, and to reflect upon their place in a loving Heavenly Father's plan.

Christ said that no sparrow falls to the ground without the Father's notice. You should foster that world view in every way you can in your congregation of God's family.

As leaders of the household of God you will do well to stress the simple, honest, face-to-face interactions of members. Members challenge each other in a humble, tentative questioning way, and enjoy sharing God's learnings and leadings from their lives. They pitch in and help each other with gardening, repainting their homes, baby-sitting, housecleaning, moving, care of the sick, repairing a car, trimming a hedge, mending clothes, entertaining guests, and an infinite number of burden-bearing experiences. While they work together they may spontaneously burst into the singing of songs the congregation knows from memory. Such working is "love made visible" and it often rescues lives from boredom and loneliness. Working together on a congregational project is a festive occasion, especially if members are "intentional neighbors" to one another.

The church family should be much more than a substitute extended family for those not fortunate enough to have wholesome human families. God's family is the basic, fundamental family even for those whose human families are good.

Suggested Readings

Parallel readings you might find helpful to supplement the

ideas in this chapter include David Switzer, *The Minister as Crisis Counselor,* Abingdon Press, 1974; and Abraham Schmidt, *The Art of Listening with Love,* Word Books, 1977.

Discussion Suggestions

Evaluate the different ways gift discernment has happened in your own lives, and consider ways it may be implemented in your congregation. Try to formulate a proposal you feel will meet your congregation's unique needs for gift discernment and which you could bring to a members' meeting.

6

Organize Around Nuclear Families

One of your goals as leaders of God's household is to run the whole congregation as you would a household of seven. You want the collective body to have within it the face-to-face reality of the primary group. Even as Christ worked in and through a 12-member group (although He was also serving the larger groups and even the whole world) you will be wise to organize your congregational life around small "nuclear family" groups of 10 to 15 adults. These "nuclear family" groups while known by a variety of titles; for example, small groups, house churches, cluster groups, house fellowships, and so forth, describe the same reality. These terms are used interchangeably in this chapter and in this volume. (See Appendix B, "The Congregation as the Family of God," for a suggested organizational model.)

Small Groups Are Like Your Nuclear Families
A. Aspects of church reality which happen best in the house fellowship include:
　　1. Hearing the testimony of the "confessing person" (Matthew 16:18) and affirming his or her readiness for baptism.
　　2. Binding and loosing as members help one another to follow Jesus in life (Matthew 18:17).

3. Greeting brothers and sisters and confronting one another in admonition and discipline (1 Timothy 6:10).

4. Forgiving one another after failures (basin and towel, John 13:14), declaring absolution, in a vital fellowship of service and forgiveness.

5. Specific day-by-day caring, sharing food, bearing one another's burdens, engaging in fellowship evangelism.

6. Discerning and affirming gifts by which the Holy Spirit creates the body (1 Corinthians 12:18, 23).

7. Praying for one another during "sendings" or prayers for healing (James 5:14).

8. Giving and receiving counsel concerning ethical issues encountered in the world.

9. Assisting one another in problems related to personal faith and faithfulness, vocational choice, marriage, change of jobs, retirement, etc.

10. Enriching family living through times of recreation, nature study, picnics, and wholesome fun on an intergenerational basis. The house fellowship may be wise to hold two kinds of services—one for fellowship and one for serious discussion and decision.

11. Banding together to move out in evangelism, establishing a new house fellowship in another area, or expanding by planned division.

(The area of mutual support of the individual and the group are discussed further in Appendix C, "Support in a Face-to-Face Group.")

The Congregation Is Like Your Extended Family

B. Aspects of churchly reality which are best mediated through the great congregation gathered in the meetinghouse include:

1. The larger congregation can provide balance, as the "multitude of counselors" with their wisdom. Small groups tend to suffer from one-sidedness (3 John 9). Seldom can an intense small group avoid bias, narrowness, or what group dynamics researchers call "group think."

2. The gifts God's Spirit places first seem to be given to the great congregation. These include the equipping ministry of the apostle, prophet, evangelist, pastor-teacher (Ephesians 4:11). It appears that God's Spirit placed these first (1 Corinthians 12:28) and does so repeatedly (1 Timothy 1:18).

3. The great congregation helps decide when small groups disagree (Acts 15).

4. The great congregation can ignite the inspiration for festivals, celebrations, thanksgivings, baptisms, covenant renewal, eucharists, protests, missionary thrusts, and mass evangelism.

5. The great congregation can provide exposition, teaching of the meaning of the Scriptures, and God's mighty acts so that the pilgrim people can find their place in history.

6. The great congregation can train for and administer programs of relief, social action, mission, prophetic witness to principalities, and cooperate with the agencies of worldwide relief, mission, and action.

7. The great congregation can engage in interchurch conversation and fellowship.

Nuclear and Extended Families Complement One Another

1. Great congregations using large meetinghouses can seek to grow to a size of 250 to 400 members. Small fellowships should consider banding together to form a great congregation for mutual strengthening.

2. All members can hold a single membership expressed in two levels of churchly reality: in the great congregation, and in a house fellowship which stands in a satellite and supporting relationship.

3. The name "church" can be reserved for membership and participation in the total churchly reality, both house fellowship and the great congregation.

4. Churchwide agencies can correspond with and relate primarily to the great congregation. Paul wrote letters to the great congregation—at Ephesus, Philippi, Rome, or Thessalonica—rather than to every individual house fellowship. Ob-

viously he sought to avoid the very real possibility of every house fellowship going its independent way. The same concern should be deeply felt today. Small groups need cross-referencing with one another.

5. Each great congregation can be led by a team with a chief "Servant-of-the-Word," assisted by helpers or elders, one selected by each house fellowship. The chief "Servant-of-the-Word" should be ordained, whereas elders might be suitably commissioned for their assignment. Ordination serves to symbolize the centrality of the Scriptures and their teaching.

6. The decisions about major policies, sanctions, positions, prophetic pronouncements, and so forth can be agreed upon by the great congregation gathered in the meetinghouse. The house fellowships may initiate discussion and submit proposals or serve as a task-force for study.

7. Serious cases of discipline should be referred by the house fellowship, by and through their elder, to the leadership team and the great congregation for action.

8. Love-feasts can be held in the small house fellowship as often and as spontaneously as the Spirit moves, while the more liturgical Lord's Supper should be observed in the great congregation gathered in the meetinghouse. Washing of the saints' feet may well be observed along with the house fellowship love-feasts.

9. Instruction of new believers (judging a person to be faithful to the Lord) and recommending him or her for baptism can be done by the house fellowship preferably using common materials used by the congregation. The actual baptizing should be in charge of the elders and the house fellowship but performed in the midst of the great congregation.

10. Scrutinizing of one another's budgets and endorsing one another's giving intentions can be done in the house fellowship, but adoption of the congregational budget can be done in the great congregation after all the elders have brought in their report of the giving intentions of house fellowship members.

11. Church letters can be forwarded by the central office of the congregation, with the approval of all of the elders; but the

actual letter, which includes a description of the member's gifts for ministry, should be countersigned by at least two thirds of the members of his or her house fellowship.

12. The worship services of the house fellowship can emphasize . sharing, praise, testimonies, decision-making, spontaneous mutual aid, love-feasts, spiritual songs, laying-on-hands, prayers for healing, giving and receiving of admonition, Bible study, intercessory prayer sessions, evangelistic conversation, mutual forgiveness and reconciliation, and hearing and discussing reports from the great congregation or church agencies. The worship services of the great congregation should emphasize expository preaching, choral readings, the use of majestic hymns and massed choirs, recital of creeds or confessions of faith, formulation of words of prophetic appeal to persons in power, festivals appropriate to the Christian calendar, receiving of missionary challenge, evangelistic appeal, and hearing reports from house fellowships.

13. Each member should attend at least two services of worship per week: one objective, ordered worship service in the great congregation; and one service of a more intimate and subjective character held in the house fellowship. The fellowship group may meet either during the Sunday school hour or on Sunday evening, or on a weekday evening in the home of one of the members. The Sunday morning hour can be reserved for the worship of the great congregation in the meetinghouse and for Christian education experiences for children. Each congregation can decide its schedule and the constituent house fellowships can decide their own schedule.

14. Because of the very heavy agenda of churchly realities which should occur in the small group of house fellowship, its services should be at least one and one-half-hours in length. The great congregation's worship might be attempted in an hour, but more time will be required if and as all of the house fellowships send in their reports and suggestions.

15. The initiative for linking house fellowships and the great congregation should rest with equal urgency upon both. Every

house fellowship should be reminded that it is in danger of becoming schismatic if it does not seek linkage with a great congregation. Likewise every great congregation should feel the imperative to reach out to welcome emerging fellowships, recent converts, immigrant groups of believers which are in the area, and to promise to take seriously any messages the house fellowship sends in. House fellowships should not merely seek ties with other small groups like themselves. House fellowships can organize their own inner life according to the gifts discerned in their midst.

16. Officers of the district conference can be given a mandate to help house fellowships and great congregations to work out a happy two-way flow of mutual support, admonition, interaction, discernment, and a program of united action.

17. Buildings, supplies, equipment, etc., can be under the administrative oversight of a resources committee of the large congregation, with constant concern that facilities are freely shared so that all possible funds can go to serve the poor and further world evangelism.

18. Membership records, including the location of each member in a house fellowship, should be maintained by the central office of the great congregation. Invalids, shut-ins, or others unable to attend meetinghouse or house fellowship services should be the special concern of the leadership team and of the house fellowships and provision be made for their nurture and fellowship.

19. Persons who desire only the great congregation experiences held in the meetinghouse, and who for any reason do not wish to be a part of a house fellowship, should be the special concern of the leadership team. It may be that a less demanding and less revealing type of traditional prayer meeting can be arranged for them until they gain courage and readiness to venture into a house fellowship. After all, many of the successes being reported by house fellowships are those which serve primarily young people and their peers. Forming house fellowships which include the life-span will likely be more difficult. Both the great

congregation and the house fellowship shall be concerned about the Christian education of youth and children and each provide that portion which is best suited to that setting.

20. Funerals should be in charge of the leadership team of the congregation with special testimonies from the deceased person's house-fellowship members. The sustained concern and listening love which grieving survivors always need can become the concern of the house fellowship.

21. Weddings should be in charge of the leadership team of the great congregation with special involvement of house fellowship members as this may be most appropriate. The great congregation may well appoint task forces to work at the strengthening of marriage relationships. House fellowships can seek to give counsel as they are able so that marriage may be truly a churchly experience.

22. The leadership team can offer leadership in long-range planning, in organizational development, in leadership development, in suggesting the person for the ordained "Servant-of-the-Word," and in coming to the aid of a house fellowship which experiences serious crisis.

23. The Congregational Ministries office of the denomination may well give counsel to small fellowships which emerge far removed from other house fellowships in order that they might find ways of banding together into a great congregation. The Board might well give continued study to the division of churchly activity between the small house fellowship and the great congregation.

Your clusters or house churches should provide a time for each member to report in. Some groups call this "check-in" time. Each member reports how his or her own walk with God is going. Members of any good family care about all of the affairs of one another's lives.

Members Report to Their Small Group

In the Book of Acts, the groups did not gather for fellowship merely because they were bored with loneliness and estrangement, or wanted to meet all of the clan. The church did not offer a chance to climb socially, by mingling with the best people of the town. One does not sense that a feeling of duty, or love and loyalty for the pastor, or dull habit brought believers together. Even the blessed ministry of mutual confession and forgiveness was not the most prominent motive.

Believers gathered to report in. They did not merely flee into one another's arms like frightened refugees. Rather they gathered like a football team going into huddle, to share signals and get directions for the next play. Sometimes they needed to meet the Master, and cry out, "Lord, why could not we cast him out?" Sometimes they wanted to rehearse all that God had done through them. Christians need to mingle because these diverse experiences need to be shared.

In the Book of Acts, Christians gathered to discuss how to relate to persecutors (4:23); to bring the gifts of money needed in the church program (5:1-10); to proclaim and expound more of the meaning of Christ's words and deeds (5:42); to choose and charge leaders (6:2-6); to help seekers to receive the Holy Spirit's fuller work (8:14-15); to hear and test the testimony of a new believer (9:27-28); to cope with the reality of the death of a member (9:38-41); to share the whole gospel with seekers (10:27-45); to be taught more fully (11:26); to pray for members in trouble (12:12); to discern a brother's call to a specific ministry (13:1-4); to confirm the souls of disciples (14:22); to select and send fraternal delegates to a conference meeting (15:2); to study an apostolic epistle (15:30); to pray together (16:16); to comfort believers (16:40); to consort with believers (17:4); to receive further blessings of the Holy Spirit (19:1-7); to say farewell to a missionary (20:1); to break bread and observe the Lord's Supper (20:7); to listen to a missionary's report (20:17); to offer counsel to a missionary (21:8-14); to declare what God had wrought (21:19); to encourage a missionary (28:14-15); and to hear Apostolic teaching (28:39). Compare these 25 reasons for gathering with the last twenty-five meetings reported in your church bulletin. Is there a stark difference?

Try to imagine taking an unsaved friend along to the twenty-five gatherings noted above, and ask whether meetings and fellowship like this has convicting power! Present-day believers need to gather for these same reasons. Too few believe that God's Spirit works in mighty power in the local assembly. Congregations must become places where believers get counsel about real problems of faithfulness to Christ. Church leaders and teachers need to demonstrate by their lives, and priorities in personal agendas, that they take the local fellowship group with supreme seriousness. Christ still promises His presence in a unique way where disciples meet in His name with the foregone view that they will do His will if they can only discern what it is. The Holy Spirit, who promises to lead disciples on in Christ's truth, waits to find those who will take the Spirit-driven fellowship seriously. Almost every fresh blessing of the Holy Spirit recorded in the New Testament came in a gathered situation.

Furthermore, the Holy Spirit's gifts for ministering (sometimes called charismatic gifts) are also designed to increase the group's power in evangelism. As the charismatic enablement comes upon one brother after another during the discussion period, the unsaved visitor is strangely convicted. As every member prophesies, the unbeliever may be moved to cry out in his confrontation with the living Christ Himself, "Surely God is among you in truth" (1 Corinthian 14:25). Group fellowship which is blessed by the Holy Spirit's distribution and redistribution of ministry gifts can lay bare the secrets of the hearts of the unbelievers.

Small Groups Set Their Own Agendas

Your small groups or clusters can be encouraged to select their own agenda, designed to meet their needs as they seek to help each other follow Jesus. As leaders you may need to provide facilitators or temporary leaders to new groups willing to try to "be church" together. You may need to keep before your people some suggestions on the creative uses of their hours together. You will likely have some who have never experienced an honest group in which persons share something that is important and precious to them. All they have known is the superficial group which "does the four G's—giggle, gabble, gobble, and git."

You should become familiar with the literature about prayer groups, growth groups, integrity groups, communication groups, life groups, enrichment groups. Society has developed literally scores of "anonymous groups" ("Alcoholics Anonymous, Diabetics Anonymous, etc.) for mutual support. Sometimes "the children of this world are wiser than the children of light." You might glean ideas that you can utilize in the mutual support groups of your congregation.

Face-to-face groups can practice mutual prayer, mutual Bible study, mutual discipling, or mutual search for light and leading around an area crucial for Christian living. They can read and discuss great books of devotion or of ethics. Some groups discipline themselves to learn the holy art of experiencing "live silence" together.

Groups can sing, play, share, and learn together. After members have learned the simpler and less demanding activities, some may be ready to go deeper in "spiritual formation." Some share personal goals for growth, and then report to the group their actual progress toward these goals, and welcome feedback and admonition from the group. The goal of "spiritual formation" is "so that the life of Christ may be formed within."

Certain Problems Tend to Reappear

Even after years of experience in a congregation which has been organized along the lines which the foregoing material in this chapter advocates, certain problems will persist. You will be wise, as congregational leaders, to work to offset and correct these problems as you organize your congregation around face-to-face house churches or clusters.

You should be aware that if clusters and house churches grow and new committed, face-to-face groups thrive, then you may sense a decline in interest in the men's brotherhood, the woman's missionary groups, and even the Sunday schools. Be prepared for this and don't panic. Expect some to lament this trend.

You will need to work endlessly at the problem of the outsider who chooses not to belong to the clusters, prayer groups, cells, or house churches around which your congregation is organized. You dare not turn against them, take an "us" versus "them" attitude, or hint that they are less spiritual than those involved in small groups. Some may be prophetic souls, unique individualists, or simply persons who dislike face-to-face groups. You should love them, honor their feelings, use their gifts in ways they enjoy serving, and find ways that they can belong and feel accepted too. Invite them to organize and help to lead in more traditional Bible studies, prayer meetings, singing groups, creative new ministries, or whatever will meet their gifts and needs.

You will need great tact and statesmanship if you are to help groups to disband and its members to regroup from time to time. While demanding an upset-the-fruit-basket reshuffling every year or two will not do, grinding on and on as an exclusive clique can be deadly too. Seek ways to make membership vital and yet make it possible and acceptable to change membership fairly easy. Honor regroupings which occur because a new "mission" or outward journey calls people to new action. Honor regrouping to swarm, and to grow larger through loving division.

Because of rapid mobility, the small groups of your congregation will find members moving away until only a small remnant is left. Two such groups can be encouraged to merge and to form a new group. If each remnant has dearly loved traditions of "how we do things," this will require maturity and patience for remnants of two groups to merge. They will be wise to begin having informal fellowship occasions together, and gradually to move to deeper levels in which they can compare their covenants and ideals about what the group ought to be and to do. On the other hand, merging the remnants of two deeply committed groups may be harder to achieve than for each remnant to keep inviting new people into their group until it is up to the desired size (12 to 15 adults) again.

Suggested Readings

For further readings in this area you may find some help in Philip and Phoebe Anderson's *The House Church,* Abingdon Press, 1975 (O.P.), and Charles M. Olson's *The Base Church,* Forum House, 1973.

Discussion Suggestions

What percentage of your members are already enjoying a face-to-face group experience in which they help one another to follow Christ? How can the congregation offer incentive and focuses of interest and concern which will enlist those currently uninvolved in a face-to-face group?

7

Claim First Loyalty for the Extended Family of God

If you are successful in getting small groups going in your congregation, you will likely find that some will go "gung-ho" for small groups. They will become intoxicated with the joys, satisfactions, and fulfillment they find in a small group which helps them to live out their Christian discipleship. As a result some may downplay the importance of the great congregation.

Defend the Great Congregation Against Its Critics

But as congregational leaders you need to insist upon the importance of the great congregation. You will need to defend it against its critics and give high priority to maximizing its fullest potential. You will want to help the great congregation to concentrate upon doing well precisely those things it can do better than the small group can. It is true that the great congregation carries the financial responsibility for maintaining a special building, but it is well worth the cost.

Youth Need the Peer Group the Congregation Can Provide

The great congregation can draw together a peer group for teenagers, and help them to move through the decisions they need to be making. Few small groups have enough fellowship for teenagers and teenagers may drift away from the church precisely for this reason. Most teenagers do not feel comfortable in an intergenerational group unless several of the teenagers can be in it together. The courtship opportunities teenagers seek can rarely be found within a small group. Recreational activities which youth enjoy are hard for a small group to provide.

Rely upon the Congregation to Provide a Balance

The great congregation can counterbalance the one-sidedness a small group so often develops, and help to overcome the lopsided "group-think" which results when too small a group achieves a too-convinced unity. The congregation is more able to provide two-sided study conferences on crucial issues. The congregation ultimately decides the legitimacy of the small groups within it.

The great congregation has the resources needed to launch programs of service for the retarded, the migrants, the blind, the deaf, the alcoholics, the refugees, the prisoners, the aged, or others needing specialized care. The small group can do some in these areas, but needs broader cooperation to make an impact.

Let the Congregation Enrich Fellowship and Worship

The great congregation can provide the stately, majestic, liturgical "Thou-centered" worship which Christians need at times. Congregations can celebrate the church year with beauty and power, enlist massive choirs which make an impact, and give depth to Christian praise that no small group can ever do. The very enriching subjective worship of the small group needs the objective worship of the great congregation to complete it.

The congregation can speak prophetic words and pleas to those in power, and throw its weight on the side of justice. The congregation can carry through programs of missions, nurture, and evangelism which are beyond the strength of the small group.

Larger congregations are more able to appeal to all ages and to provide an intergenerational fellowship. Singles need the opportunities the congregation can offer. Those who have never been married, those who have experienced divorce, or those left alone by the death of a spouse—all need the one-hundredfold fathers and mothers and brothers and sisters which Christ promised that His family will provide.

Help the Congregation Relate to the Denomination

You can help your congregation to keep vitally linked to the denomination of which you are a part. You can see to it that informational and promotional mailings do not end up in the wastebasket but actually get to the persons for whom they were intended. You can invite denominational leaders into your congregation so that face-to-face acquaintance can happen.

You can send messages from your congregation to your denominational offices. If God has led you to consensus on an issue, denominational leaders should know about it. If programs and literature they advocate work well, you should tell them so. If their ideas are bookish or remote, you should tell them this too. Denominational servants can drift into a very remote lingo and into irrelevant programs if local congregational realities do not offer a mid-course correction from time to time.

The Congregation Needs the Small Group

Sometimes persons who work all week within institutions (especially church institutions) are pretty fed up with structures, large meetings, boards, budgets, and organizational tedium by the time Sunday comes. Often they want only a face-to-face group for their fellowship on Sunday. They may drag their feet about the organized congregation and its formal programs. They may over-idealize primary relationships.

As congregational leaders you will need to understand where such persons are coming from. You will need courage to level with them and insist that they try to conquer their feelings. The congregation needs them and they need the congregation.

You as leaders of the congregations should be active in a small group yourselves, preferably each of you in a different one.

By example, public statement, and in every way possible you will be wise to affirm the good effects which warm group life tends to bring into the larger congregation. Watch for these signs of "family."

You may well rejoice when you sense first names and pet names being used intergenerationally. Be glad when you sense that a grandpa knows about some small lad's puppy. Smile when you see loving admonition happening throughout the congregation. Rejoice when spontaneous mutual aid moves swiftly to meet need, when reconciliation happens on a daily basis, when hand-me-downs of worn but usable clothing appear on growing children of struggling families, and when grandparents, whose children are far away, are taken in and loved.

Suggested Readings

For further readings in the area of concern discussed in this chapter, you may find helpful the book by Joseph McCabe, *The Power of God in a Parish Program,* Westminster Press, 1959, (O.P.); and James D. Glasse's book *Putting It Together in the Parish,* Abingdon Press, 1972.

Discussion Suggestions

Examine the ways you are enabling your small groups to cooperate in the total congregational program. Is your congregation specializing in doing well what small groups cannot do? If competition, rather than cooperation, has begun to emerge between the small groups and the entire congregation, what can you do to correct it?

8

Commission Some Family Members for Ministry

In the process of gift discernment your congregation may likely have pointed out several persons with the gift of teaching. You may commission them to confer and serve the congregation as its Nurture Commission.

Your gift-discernment process may likely have identified several persons who have the gift of hospitality. You may commission them to serve and confer together as the Fellowship Commission of the congregation. If you have discovered several persons who have the gift of helping and healing, you may commission them to serve and lead the congregation as its Service Commission. Others with gifts of wisdom and knowledge may serve as elders. Those with the gifts of prophecy and discernment may serve on the Social Action and Evangelism Commission of the congregation.

Regard Your Leaders as Servants and Commission Them

Each Commission can be helped to select one from their number to serve as their leader. Periodically the leaders of each of these ministering commissions should meet together as a cabinet called the "Program Cabinet."

In cabinet meetings the needs of the whole congregation,

both its inner life and its outreach, are surveyed with loving care. Gaps in program are noted. Unmet needs of certain persons or age-groups are discussed and prayed about, until a sense of leading develops as to what should be done, and who "filled with the Holy Ghost, shall be placed in charge of this business" (Acts 6:3).

A few advocates of strong, centralized, efficient administration will urge that you choose only the leader of each commission by gift discernment (or even by democratic election) and that then you allow that person to handpick the rest of the commission membership. Their argument for this method is that the commission will result in a likeminded, congenial, unified, highpowered body which will get a lot done.

The pitfalls of this method are many. You will likely get what is called "administration by crony" where the dangers of bias and lopsidedness are great. A strong leader will select followers, satellites, and "yes men." If members are picked because they are already congenial and of one mind, leaders can evade the hard lesson of "radical subordination," of dialoguing to consensus with those who are noticeably different. (Radical subordination seeks a highest common denominator.)

Expect Many Ministries to Mingle

As all of these specialized ministries interact, mingle, and flow together in the life of the congregation, some of the most creative innovations become possible. Suppose your service and social action commission develops a conviction that your congregation should offer help to refugees from another country or should serve the migrant laborers nearby. All of the commissions can unite in planning an experience in which study, and service, and fellowship are blended. Your nurture commission can plan a series of intergenerational teaching sessions, tracing the refugee and migrant problems in the Scripture, with the constant refrain of God's care for Israel during her helpless migrant-refugee years. Grandparents can tell the story of the refugee years when forefathers settled in this country. The fellowship commission can plan refugee meals, and sharing sessions when local migrant-refugees are brought in. The whole flow of experiences can climax with action proposals for the church.

Each of your commissions can begin to see themselves as a smaller "system" within the larger congregational "system." Because of the hours they spend together focusing upon the task that is theirs, commission members can develop strong emotional ties to one another. By wrestling together about common problems, and sharing ideas for one another's testing, they can grow beyond the "brainstorming" stage. They can experience the "forming" stage as shared goals emerge. If they "hang-in-there" with openness and honesty, they can begin to feel the awe and power of the "norming" stage. During this stage "norms," standards, guidelines, and convictions become commonly held and cherished. After the "norming" stage has done its work, the group is ready to move on into the "performing" stage. (For further description of the congregation as a system, see Appendix D, "Shepherding the Congregation as a Living System.")

Avoid Competition and Overlap

Your "program cabinet" can call for biblical studies focused upon one issue or problem area and assign the pastor and the nurture commission the task of carrying through with these studies. The cabinet can weigh the discontent and need in an area of congregational life and agree upon the guidelines and policies needful to strengthen any new program. The cabinet can be alert for overlap or competition of interests and programs in the congregation. The cabinet can call for budget provisions to make a good program possible, assign responsibility for carrying it out, and agree upon criteria to evaluate progress made in solving the problem.

The cabinet which commands an overview of all congregational life can be alert for balance. Cabinet members can secure two-sided coverage of issues, and protest if some person or cause is being treated unfairly. The cabinet can help the various commissions to keep their goals clear, their programs moving, their decision-making fair and their gains integrated. The cabinet can help the congregation to keep focusing toward attainable goals in the future.

Scrutinize Your Family's Way of Working Together

Just because your congregation is God's household, rejoicing in the unities of one Lord, one faith, one baptism, one God and Father, etc., is no reason to assume that administration does not need scrutiny, and that methods of working together do not need improving. Because your spiritual ideals are so high it is extremely important that your process be scrutinized and tested for consistency.

You may secure someone with gifts in administration to function as a "process observer," sitting in on selected meetings of the program cabinet, and offering them feedback at the close about just what went on. If a few persons tried to function as a power-bloc, they need to be rebuked. If anyone has loaded the information circuits unfairly this needs to be pointed out. If readiness was ignored, the matter of timing must be faced. If undue pressures were brought upon a minority, this needs to be called to the cabinet's attention. If crucial issues are allowed to remain "under the table," this tendency should be noted.

Has the cabinet been fair to the traditions of the congregations and the convictions of some older members? Have the "prophets" and the advocates for change been sensitive to the feelings of silent members? Is there behavior which might grieve the Spirit of God who should be "dictator" of the meeting? Have emotion-loaded words been overused?

Were parallel ideas linked by summary statements so that members could trace an emerging consensus? Were the meaning of key terms kept clear? Was the cabinet helped to count the cost of proposals for change? Did everyone seem to sense that the conclusion and proposal for action was indeed something which seemed good to the Holy Spirit and to us?

Suggested Readings

Helpful for further reading on the issues raised in this

chapter are books like the one by Arthur Adams, *Pastoral Administration,* Westminster Press, 1964 (O.P.), and another by Jim Wallis, *Agenda for Biblical People,* Harper and Row, 1976.

Discussion Suggestions

Are all of your commissions (or committees charged with action) necessary? Is there duplication and overlap? If your members are already overloaded with committee meetings, could any existing house church or prayer group or cluster be asked to assist them? Examine your congregation's structure for simplicity and flow of ideas.

9
Make Decisions Carefully

Jesus thanked His Father that He hid some things from the wise and prudent and revealed them to the babes and children. This identity as God's Son, on the inner and confidential circle of sharing with God, was a crucial part of Christ's self-identity. Your members should have some of this feeling too.

The way that you decide things together will reveal a great deal about the kind of household of God you really are. Just ask yourselves in all honesty—"How important were the last ten issues we decided together as a congregation?" and "How much like God's family were the methods we used to reach a decision?"

Often congregations fail in being God's household together because the real issues are never consciously faced, but are allowed to decide themselves by default. Profound issues of Christian ethics are regarded as too hot to handle. The congregation decides little except matters of budget, buildings, or hiring and firing a pastor! Many of your members seem to want it that way, and will resist if you urge that your congregation try to come to an agreement upon issues of profound importance.

Avoid Using Parliamentary Process
Your members may come from their participation in sec-

ular organizations all week and assume that, since parliamentary process works everywhere else, it should be used with God's household—the church. You will need clear theological thinking and quiet courage to withstand this expectancy and unverbalized pressure.

Your members may favor deciding things as the Queen's Parliament does because they are not aware that there might be another way. All that they have ever known is reliance upon a democratic majority, determined by a secret ballot.

Admit That Parliamentary Process Has Some Merits

In all fairness to the parliamentary method, or Parliamentary Law, or to Roberts Rules of Order, it does have a few strengths, and it can be used for small issues, or for large meetings in which a decision simply has to be reached quickly.

Parliamentary process insists that a motion be placed before the assembly, and this does help to get the issue out into the open, stated clearly, so that discussion can be focused. You can be assured that at least two persons want the issue as stated, because a motion requires a second. The process insures that only one thing will be on the floor at a time, that the minority will get a fair hearing, and that they can record their objection in a negative-minority vote, thus saving face.

Parliamentary process insures that the numerical majority will win, and keeps a vocal minority from delaying a decision forever. It can prevent stalemates, deadlocks, delaying tactics, and the tyranny of a few "cranks." Some church members like it because they can debate each other furiously during the time they are acting like a parliament and then be good buddies and brothers afterward because their disagreement dissolved after the majority spoke its will.

The greatest reason some of your church members will favor the parliamentary process is that "our government uses it and it works," our business firms use it and they "succeed," and we should use it too in order to be at home in our culture.

Members who urge reasons like this reveal that they have

not taken seriously the deep and fundamental differences between God's household and secular agencies. Even the human family would not use motions, amendments, counter motions, and "counting of noses" to reach a good family decision. Much more the church should be very reserved about using this process.

Tell Your People Why You Wish to Limit Its Use

As leaders of God's household you will want to teach against the overuse of parliamentary process for some of the following reasons. It assumes that the majority is right, whereas in "holy history" (the history of God's people) the lonely prophet was often right even though he was in the minority. The use of motions and the limiting of discussion to the motion as stated often narrows down the issue too soon and slants the discussion prematurely. The very nature of the process tends to polarize the thinking into a yes or no, right or wrong, two-option pattern. Larger, holistic, and consensus thinking is often inhibited.

Because motions and "calling for the question" can often force a vote, the process provides a way for a congregation to move on without patient listening to the dissenting, prophetic brother or sister. The radical subordination which should exist in God's household can be bypassed. Parliamentary process may solve a brother's or sister's conscience that it is right to ride roughshod over the convictions of another brother or sister in the church. It tends to produce a cold atmosphere of competition, expediency, legalism, and compromise, suitable to the areas of secular politics. It makes more difficult the mood of reverent worship in which God's people should conduct all of their business meetings. Decision-making within God's family should be an act of worship.

Even more serious for God's household, parliamentary process quickly becomes so complex and intricate (as amendments add to amendments and privileged motions only are in order) that the average church member gets confused and tangled up in the process. Subtly the highly educated and the bureaucrats who have mastered the legalistic details get their way, because the less educated lapse into silence. A victorious majority vote then pretends to put the stamp of a heavenly Father's approval upon all of that disunity and triumph of the strong, smart, and slick operator over the weak, less educated, or less experienced.

Try for Consensus

The way God's family came to consensus at Jerusalem as recorded in Acts 15 may be a model. It appears that James sensed that, because all of the announced changes of mind, and all the testimonies of God's leading were pointing in the same direction, and the new-light from the Scriptures were endorsing this direction, it was time to "try for consensus." Somehow probably by the nodding of heads, smiles, sighs of glad relief, and other "body language," people let it be known that they were agreeing.

Consensus was achieved because "it seemed good to all." This is repeated in verse 22, verse 25, and again in verse 28. Consensus did not mean that no one had any quiet reservations. It meant that they were ready to go along, gladly and freely, in the direction which Holy Spirit action, brotherly convictions, and scriptural insights were pointing. They put their consensus into writing, but they were careful not to try to claim too much, or to spread it out into a lot of legalistic demands. They stated their consensus in terms of "minimal agreements," just these "few necessary things." They were sensitive to the feelings of those whose mind was so recently changed, and careful not to lay their new consensus upon other people "as a burden" (vv. 23-29).

Consensus was attributed to the Holy Spirit's action but this did not render unimportant such commonsense procedures as two-sided presentation, search for new evidence, respect for their traditions, humility of leaders to admit that their mind had changed, claiming the middle ground of shared agreements, and stating their consensus in "minimum" terms, rather than maximum ones. (See Appendix E, "Methods Which May Grieve the Holy Spirit and Prevent a Spirit-Driven Consensus," and F, "Some Considerations Related to Group Decision-Making," for further consideration of consensus and decision-making.)

Alternate Input and Discussion

Some congregations try to solve problems and decide issues just by having a series of sermons devoted to the problem followed by a secret ballot vote. This method fails to develop real unity because members do not really hear one another. Persons often do not take ownership of a decision which they did not help to make.

Other congregations hurry at once to talk-it-over discussions, inviting everyone to share what they have always thought. All too often this pools a vast amount of prejudice and ignorance, and the resulting decision may be a weak least-common-denominator one.

A congregation of 160 members faced a difficult decision when a 45-year-old sister asked whether she could go on serving as a leader in the congregation even though she had secretly married a divorced man who was a nominal Roman Catholic. She asserted that she was willing to ask forgiveness for her sin of failing to "give and receive counsel from the church" as she had promised to do in her vow of believer's baptism. She did not regard living as wife with a previously divorced man as living in sin.

The leadership team arranged for both scriptural studies and input to be alternated with small-group discussion. One sermon probed God's intentions about marriage. A second sermon expounded God's ways when His family failed to obey His highest will.

All the congregation was convened in groups of about twelve adults, and a recording secretary or "clerk of the meeting" was chosen to bring the small-group's consensus back to a congregational meeting. After all these reports were heard by the congregation, in a meeting in which the married-in-secret sister was present, the moderator summarized the emerging consensus.

The elders later brought this back as a specific proposal. The congregation accepted it as their position. Both unity and conviction were strengthened by this procedure.

Involve Your Heavenly Father in Your Decisions

To lead your congregation through honest disagreement, vigorous debate, and announced changes of mind, to a consensus which "seems good to the Holy Spirit and to us," you will need to come yourselves to a deep conviction that your heavenly Father is deeply involved when His household is trying to decide a problem in line with His will. Paul told Timothy that, when leading a household of God decision-making session, he was "in the presence of God and of Christ and of the elect angels," and should beware of any favoritisms or partiality which could not endure heavenly scrutiny (1 Timothy 5:21-22).

This coincides with Christ's warning that leaders "do not despise one of these little ones; for I tell you that in heaven their angels always behold the face of my Father who is in heaven" (Matthew 18:10). Christ further said that any binding and loosing which a group of His followers make here on earth was to be done simultaneously and in correlation with what heaven itself is binding and loosing (Matthew 18:18). He promised that the decision-making situation will bring theophany and a sense of His divine presence. "When you are gathered in My Name, to discover My mind and will about a matter, there am I in the midst" (Matthew 18:19-20). Your decision-making triumphs should be some of the most sacred occasions of worship which you ever experience in the congregation.

As you lead God's household toward consensus, you reassert your childlike faith that God's Spirit already has one mind about the problem, and is willing to reveal it, if His people meet the conditions. You may be wise to call your people together in this confidence, ready to enter deeply into the search for God's mind on the matter, to repent of proud individualisms, to experience radical subordination to one another, and to build upon the contribution of each previous speaker.

You can encourage the congregation to believe that the full group's wisdom is better than the partial grasp of truth which any one member possesses. You can call upon participants to listen deeply to one another with the loving intensity with which God listens to their prayers. You can claim the readiness of God's Spirit to energize any charismatic gifts of Holy Spirit discernment, wisdom, knowledge, prophesy, or of teaching which are needed to solve the issues then and there.

Intervene Tactfully to Help the Group Reach Its Decisions

You can help the timid persons to be heard. You can challenge the overly talkative persons to give everyone a chance. You can summarize progress being made. You can gladly announce when and how your own mind is changing, you can notice carefully the direction in which all of the announced changes of mind are pointing, you can call the group to times of incubation in silent prayer, you can help to test the proposals for solution which start to be offered. You can join the group in glad worship when God's Spirit leads someone to make the proposal which really seems good to the Holy Spirit and to us.

Offer Training Classes in Group Process and Leadership

Because your ability to decide important matters together is so extremely important if you are to remain a faithful church, you may be well advised to secure some training sessions, for yourselves and your people, in the art of group process and leadership. This type of training is just as important as training in nurture or in evangelism.

Through your training sessions you can seek to help all of your members to become aware of the importance of clearly defining a problem, the skill of generating possible solutions, the ways to weigh and test possible solutions until the best one is found, ways to facilitate an emerging consensus, and ways to plan to implement a chosen solution. Your people may idealize consensus, but not know some of the useful ways to help it to happen.

In your training sessions you can sharpen your members' awareness of functions someone needs to perform if the group is to have inner cohesion. Someone needs to clarify terms and standards, to help to relieve tensions which mount unduly, encourage the timid to participate, be deeply aware of belief strengths, be sensitive to areas of tenderness, absorb some hostility at times, use humor skillfully, mediate differences, restate goals, reflect back feelings, sense obstacles yet to be overcome, and help to keep the search issue-centered rather than person-centered. Such skills are needed to keep the group process at a high level.

You can utilize feedback tools, group observer outlines, and leader-rating scales in developing both your own tact and skill as leaders, and to upgrade the group work of your members. Your congregational decision-making will be enriched if you and your members increase skills in making assertions, in asking questions, in securing facts, in testing facts for accuracy, and in securing two-sided coverage of an issue. The common sense and caring of your people will go a long way, but you can all profit by some practical pointers. Your peers can give you honest feedback on how well you initiate, how friendly you seem, how skillfully you rephrase, how tactfully you link the remarks of others, how insightfully you summarize progress, and how wisely you time your proposed solutions. (See Appendix G, "Group Building and Task Functions"; H, "Rating a Leader's Behavior"; I, "Feedback"; J, "Was Our Committee Meeting Today Healthy or Sick?" and K, "My Participation Profile as a Group Member" for several tools to evaluate group-leader performance.)

Don't Try to Decide Too Many Problems at One Time

Part of your statesmanship as leaders will be tested by which issues you insist get major time and attention, and which issues you feel the group must simply "live with." You will be keenly aware that many crucial decisions, changes of mind, changes of standards, and changes of lifestyle are going on subformally, by slow osmosis, all the time. Many changes are being made by default because the group feared to face them openly and above board. However, not every issue needs to be decided in a church meeting. Members can join other persons of good will in changing their approach to energy conservation, pollution, car pooling, and such issues without having a congregational meeting about them, unless sharp polarities exist.

If you err on the side of trying to solve all issues by group process, and attempt to have the group help individuals solve their personal problems too, you will become too "problem oriented." You will burn up all your time and energies solving your own problems. You will likely lose your life even while you are trying to save it. Your group tone may become grim, tense, heavy, and legalistic.

If you err on the side of tackling as few problems and avoid a public show-down whenever you can, you may accumulate so many deep and important disagreements beneath the surface that your fellowship will become shallow. Your people may begin to doubt whether it really is possible for God's household to help its members to find a way to walk together in united convictions.

Rejoice in Good Mutual-Subordination

As leaders you will often be privileged to see God's children behaving like family in spontaneous ways you never intended or planned. Just as good families seldom demand verbal allegiance to abstract beliefs, or creeds, so your congregational members may rebuke heresy hunts being employed. Families don't demand that certain verbal cliches be mouthed in order to be accepted. Decisions are not made by majority vote. Bad news is kept secret in order to protect a family member. Overly tired members are given a chance to rest. It is all-right to cry if sorrow comes. Members need not always be dressed up to feel approved. Some lapses of temper are tolerated. Acts of retribution are frowned upon. Harmless jokes and tricks played on each other help to relax tensions. Foibles and fads are challenged. Selfishness is seen as a sin against the family. While each person is to be set free to grow yet each is expected to be loyal to the group. Decisions are made as part of a shared life.

Suggested Readings

Parallel readings you might find helpful in relation to deci-
sion-making include such books as Lyle E. Schaller's book, *The
Decision Makers,* Abingdon Press, 1974; Tillman Smith's
booklet, *Boards: Purposes, Organization, Procedures,* Herald
Press, 1978, paper; and Howard Brinton's Pendle Hill Pamphlet
No. 20, *Guide to Quaker Practice,* 1943, paper.

Discussion Suggestions

Discuss which basic decisions of your congregation in the
last 10 years were made by congregational study and decision,
and which by slow subformal changes. Your statesmanship will
be tested in knowing which issues to bring to the congregation
for formal decision making. Which issues do you plan to face
next year, and how will you proceed?

10

Use Team Leadership

In extended families, leadership is always shared. Many grandparents and uncles and aunts help to guide the clan. In the family of God leadership is always plural.

There are many reasons, arising from historical evidence, why you should seek to have a "team" of leaders to guide the congregation. Only a few will be cited here.

The Bible Points Toward Team Leadership

The Bible always mentions leaders in the plural, and assumes that a team of leaders share the leadership. From Exodus 18:13-27 in which Moses was told to institute a team approach, through Acts 6:1-6 in which the team of apostles instituted a second team of "deacons," to 1 Corinthians 12 and Ephesians 4 in which it is assumed that the Holy Spirit spreads out leadership gifts among many members—in each case the evidence is toward team leadership.

Furthermore, the lessons from history warn that too much power assigned to one "boss" leader tends to weaken the people and, at the same time, corrupt the leader. Too often a host of subtle errors creep in when only one person is looked to for answers—that person's presence begins to define the church, that person alone can be God's channel for sacramental grace, he or she has these rights for life and regardless of real gifts in all areas, and all other persons feel "lay" and incompetent.

Unless leadership is shared by a team the "boss-leader" may be destroyed by overwork, distracted by needing to cover-up realized incompetence, or seduced into illusions of omni-competence. The single pastor system of Protestantism usually tends to rely too heavily upon one person, and allows members to lapse into an audience. The Catholic priest too readily becomes the authoritative "father."

See Yourselves as "Elders" in the Family of God

You will be wise to rely constantly upon the ascended Lord who has promised to "rule" and to lead His church. As you assemble the congregation of "gift coveters" the Lord at the throne gives the gifts to that gathered congregation so that they can function faithfully with one another and in the world. A big part of your task will be to help the congregation to define their goals, and find their sense of direction, and mission. As leaders you should have been members of the congregation long enough to know its history, traditions, foibles, failures, as well as its potential.

You will not be wise to see yourselves as "chief rabbis" who interpret the laws or rules for your group. You will not want to function as charismatic leaders, getting fresh revelations from God in ways the others do not, and asking for personal loyalty to your decisions. Always you will want to seize the unused basin and seek to stoop to serve rather than seize power so as to rule; you will expect authority to reside in the binding-and-loosing group rather than in yourselves and will welcome rebuke and admonition from members of the congregation. Even though you are a team of leaders, you are subordinate to the congregation.

Expect That Women Will Serve on the Team

Your team should assume and expect that the Holy Spirit

will gift women for spiritual ministry. The proven services of one or more women in your congregation may possess such intrinsic authority that some women will likely be called and charged to serve on the leadership team.

Sex should not decide in what role members may serve as leaders. If gifted, called by the church, and charged for a particular service, you may have a "Priscilla" as co-worker in any one of a number of areas of ministry. You may have someone like "Phoebe" in a deaconess role. If the Holy Spirit gifts, and a woman's proven ministries are like those of Junias in Romans 16:7, who was "eminent among the apostles" (NEB), you will be wise also to give honor to whom honor is due. In the new reality "in Christ," hierarchies of slave over free, Jew over Greek, or male over female dare not exist (Galatians 3:28).

These are some basic principles to keep in mind as you lead. Yours should be a shared leadership which recognizes that there are many ministries and that assumes any one person is not equally gifted to do everything. You should assume that every member is being gifted by the ascended Christ.

Admit That You Possess Authority

You will be wise to keep in mind that, when the congregation discerns your gifts for a ministry, calls you to lead out in a ministry, charges you to serve in an appropriate office, and focuses the power of their corporate prayers upon you for your work—then some authority is actually conferred upon you by these prayers and charge. Don't pretend that you have no responsibility and authority. Just be as clear as you can just what your responsibility is, and then take up your task with a determination to be faithful in it. Expect the congregation to hold you accountable for precisely that task.

Your "track-record" of proven performance also tends to give authority to what you say and do. If the Holy Spirit has confirmed your service with signs following, and some persons are bearing testimony that God has honored your ministry to bless their lives, this will add authority to your office. But beware of allowing a "halo" of status to gather around your head unduly.

Beware of Being Boss

In the secular world the boss-subordinate, or line and staff style of leadership is common. The world expects that great ones "lord-it-over" lesser ones. But remember that your Lord has said "this shall not be so among you." You will be wise not to accord authority, prestige, or power to the person on your team who has the most training, receives the most salary, who happens to be ordained, or who happens to be male. You will naturally listen with respect to the voice of experience and give special attention to persons who have devoted much time or thought to a given issue. But mutual subordination is always your ideal. You who have served long on the leadership team may want to help to apprentice and train a young Timothy, as the Apostle Paul did his Timothy.

Your Team May Need an Administrator

The persons who are assigned a place on the team will vary according to the congregation's task in the community and its priorities for its inner life. Congregations with many young people may ask a "youth minister" to serve on the team. Congregations with a varied and challenging outreach program may have a "community visitor-worker" on the team. If the congregation is doing a great deal of its decision-making through face-to-face groups, clusters, or house fellowships, then a "congregational moderator" who coordinates the work of the clusters may serve on the team.

If the commissions of the congregation are leading vigorous programs of missions-evangelism, nurture, fellowship, stewardship, and youth activities, and also need to plan many intergenerational and congregation-wide activities in which all flows together in a holistic learning-worship-service experience, then a "congregational administrator" may need to be a part of the team. The New Testament congregations model just such a variety of leadership patterns.

Every Team Needs a Preacher-Teacher-Equipper or Pastor

Always a preacher-teacher-equipper or pastor should be part of the team. Because the Scriptures must be kept central in guiding the life of the congregation, therefore the person who is set apart, ordained, and charged to "equip-with-the-Word" must be a part of the team that leads the church. The pastor is enabler, never boss. The pastor is equipper, never the one who does things for passive people that they should really be doing. The pastor is worship leader, and needs to have access to team sharing so that corporate worship may truly express the deepest and best of all that God's Spirit is doing through all of the activities of the congregation. (See Chapter 8 in which the task of the preacher-teacher-equipper is described in more detail.)

Fit Your Team Size to Your Congregation's Needs

How large should your leadership team be? It needs to be at least two. Some who wish to divide their interests along the lines of their gathered life, and their scattered life, may have the pastor representing nurture, decision-making, fellowship, and worship (or their gathered life)—and a minister of outreach representing visitation, stewardship, evangelism, and social action. Thus the team of two could confer and attempt to correlate all of the gathered-scattered ministries of the church.

Other congregations have a pastor (who enables, preaches-teaches, counsels, and leads worship), an administrator (who correlates the work of the commissions of nurture, youth, and missions), and a moderator (who correlates the work of clusters, house fellowships, and congregational meetings). These three function as a team. Each is either supported financially or not supported according to the need each one has for financial help, the load of work each is expected to assume responsibility to do and to supervise, and the policy the congregation has concerning who gets paid for doing what and why to pay or not to pay.

Your Team Can Coordinate Program

In the team, the members can support one another and pray

for one another, find security because they are understood, coordinate their activities, and recommend agenda items which one or another commission of the church should be attending to. They can do "awareness raising" and share long-range planning.

In team meetings you can keep alert for areas of overlap and collision between subgroups of the congregation. You can observe the information flow. You can keep asking who in the congregation is being missed or ignored. You can examine the balance of money, energy, and attention each part of the work receives.

Team meetings should allow some time to see future visions and to dream dreams. Some concerns will be regular and routine. But the team should spend some time in deeper and more probing reflection as to why some problems and crises recur so regularly.

Your Team Can Set Priorities

Team meetings can engage in some "quality control" reflections. They may honestly share what each one feels about the quality of life and fellowship in the congregation, the uses of time each one is making, and how their stewardship of time relates to the deepest needs of the church. Team members can share angers, feelings of inadequacy or loneliness, and frustrations which tend to cause depressions.

Team members can help to set priorities among competing claims for time and attention, so that causes most vital to the congregational goals receive major attention. Team members can try to "cover" for one another in an emergency, and to defend one another against gossip or unfair attack.

Your Team Can Model Good Relationships

One of the weaknesses of team leadership is "cronyism." Leaders become chummy, function as a clique, and keep each other busy with meetings, memos, minutes, and talk-it-over-time. Administrators tend "to make work for each other," and may expect the church to pay their time for endless conferring with one another, while they are unwittingly getting farther away and more remote from the congregation they are trying to lead!

Suggested Readings

Books you might find helpful for further study include the one by C. W. Brister, *Pastoral Care in the Church,* Harper & Row, 1977, and the one by Robert K. Greenleaf, *Servant Leadership,* Paulist Press, 1977.

Discussion Suggestions

How did each of you now on the team get there? Why are *you* on the team and not some other servants of the congregation? Evaluate your team work. How might this be improved?

11

Hold One Another Accountable

As a leadership team of God's household, you will need to set up clear lines of accountability. Since you are not in a "line-and-staff" relationship, you can not merely assume that the person who is "boss" supervises that person under him or her. Ordinarily the person who is higher upon the ladder of power supervises the person who is subordinate. But you are peers, on one level, and equals.

Because you are "peers" and not a hierarchy, you will need great courage and determination if you are to really supervise each other. You may be wise to have a neutral person, who is well informed about supervisory practices, to help you to set up your plan of mutual supervision.

Agree to Be Accountable in Specific Areas

You may decide on a "round robin," circular pattern, in which leader A supervises leader B, leader B supervises leader C, and leader C supervises leader A. A regular schedule of supervision should be agreed upon and not left up to impulse or to chance. If the schedule and commitment to keep it are not firm, supervision will soon fizzle out. Set dates firmly, in advance, when you will meet for mutual supervision.

Specific questions should always be part of the supervisory hour. These may include the following: How are you meeting your job description? What exhibits do you have to illustrate the way you are working to meet the expectations of your assignment? What is going well? What problems are you experiencing? What specific channels have you set up to secure feedback?

How are your relationships with the specific persons with whom you must interact? How clear are your co-workers about your goals? What "critical incidents" have occurred? What specific goals have you reached in your work this past week? Analyze one crisis for your own performance in it. What overall vision guides you?

Learn a Loving Family Way of Giving Feedback

When serving as a supervisor to a co-worker, it is crucial that you step into the role and fulfill it without apology, embarrassment, or evasion. Your own turn will be coming when one of your peers will serve as your supervisor.

In giving feedback to a peer, begin with the areas in which he or she is most clearly asking for your scrutiny and honest evaluation. If a person is asking for help, you can give very honest, probing, and even revealing responses and they will not hurt the person. It is when you try to give feedback which has not been asked for that the hurt occurs easily.

Give a peer feedback as to the way you see his or her performance, and then check it out to see whether your perceptions concur with him or her. Give a peer feedback very soon after an incident occurred, and not a long while afterward. Give feedback based upon facts that you know, and not upon gossip. Give a peer feedback about matters to which he or she can respond. It is frustrating to be told "you are too tall," or "you are too short," or some other matter which the recipient is powerless to change.

In giving feedback, always be willing to check out your perceptions with other neutral and fair observers. Always give feedback in small doses, and while the person's ego-strength is strong so that solid growth and gains will result.

Keep Each Person's Job Description in Focus

In a supervisory hour keep the person's job description and goals clearly in mind, keep the facts about the person's performance clear, grasp the total situation before you offer comments, be sure that the person's level-of-trust in your caring love is high, and offer your feedback so that it facilitates personal growth. Make sure that the person is free to say "no" to it if he or she chooses.

At the highest levels, when you supervise and offer feedback to a peer, you ask, "Where is God at work in this? Who precisely are you as you function? With what skill and tact, and power, and effectiveness did you perform your ministry? Just what is going on in your situation?"

Practice Radical Subordination in God's Household

The implicit assumptions or "contract" in operation between you and your peer during these structured hours of mutual supervision ought to include confidentiality, mutual trust, mutual support, mutual reliance upon and yieldedness to God's Spirit, and mutual belief in the possibility of change and growth, with sensitive concern to preserve one another's dignity as a person.

After all, in the "household codes" of the New Testament letters, members of God's household are expected to practice a very radical supervision and mutual subordination toward one another. The subordinant persons are chosen of God to be "moral agents." A father is to be subordinant to the "courage level" of his child (Colossians 3:18—4:1). A husband is to bestow honor upon the wife whom surrounding society has decreed to be weaker (1 Peter 2:13—3:7). Children and slaves are addressed by God first, then their parents or bosses. The master, Philemon, is to let the realities of his brothering of Onesimus challenge the most deeply held slavery structures of society. It is thought that the early church used these subordination passages during catechism so that converts would grasp the radically different lifestyle within God's household.

Examine One Another's Ethics as Revealed in Leadership

As leaders of God's household, you will be wise to include in your frank and honest mutual supervision of one another precisely those subtle ethical issues and those misuses of power which most often corrupt the souls of leaders who are called to use power and influence over others. Following are sample questions about the ethics of leadership and the abuses of power which you might probe in supervising each other. (Note that it is as important to probe successes as it is "failures.")

Just who did you mean when you kept saying "they say ..." as though you were quoting some "invisible committee." Why did you try so hard to make your point? To get your way?

Why did you call your opponents idea "a dangerous precedent," whereas you thought of your own innovation as pure courage and wisdom?

When the "eyedrift" of expectancy was turning toward you and the people were "imputing power" to you by implicitly inferring that you had the wisdom and the answers, why did you "suffer it to be so now"? You grabbed the power!

Why did you rally supporters before you went into that meeting, so that you were almost sure to get your way?

Did you really mean all of those compliments you bestowed upon that person you wanted to agree with you, or was some of it flattery?

Did you use only some "selected facts," and not tell the whole truth? Did you carefully select the facts you presented in order to make your case look good?

Did you really offer some "loud protest" on a minor point in order to hide the disunity or ugly facts of a much deeper and more basic issue that you did not want to see surfaced now?

Did you "drop important names," "collect testimonials," quote authors or even Scripture texts out of context in order to make your case look stronger than it really is? What would have happened if you had made a fair, two-sided presentation? What if you had spelled out the arguments against your favored position as fully as you did those for it?

Were you really dropping into peoples minds the components of the solution you favored, so that later on one of your friends could come forward with the solution you wanted, and you could hail it as "their idea?"

Do you read all of the circumstantial evidence, all of the "handwriting on the wall" as favoring the way you want to go? Has the minority who opposed you been helped to get their case clearly presented?

Did you secure unfair advantage by using emotion-loaded words, or the skills of argument and debate to get your own way? Did you allow your opponents suggestions to be subtly ridiculed?

Did you "turn-on-the-charm" in order to "win friends and influence people" to get your own way? Did you let it appear that "the cards are stacked" in favor of the solution you favored?

When you rephrased and summarized both sides, did you upgrade your side, and play down your opposition?

Did you tolerate "hidden agendas," operations "under the table" which some of your group members would not have liked had they sensed it?

Supervise One Another to Maximize Family Realities

As congregational leaders, affirm and commend in each other those activities which increase unity, and challenge in each other those activities that destroy unity. In the constant struggle between the autonomy of the individual ego and the good of the group, you will often decide for the group, and believe that the individual will find the best fulfillment in the interpersonal relationships of a good group.

You will be wise to expect to find a rhythm of crises with a following period of euphoria. You will be church statesmen and women if you celebrate consensus when you have reached it. You will be reverent around the sense of the holy and the mystical in one another and in your congregation.

In your mutual supervision you will be most helpful if you celebrate and affirm in one another the spirit of discernment, the spirit of joy, the refusal of cliques, the completeness of forgiveness offered to the deviant, and the ability to play it cool during stress.

Suggested Readings

Books which you can read to understand more fully the nature of the supervisory process include Charles R. Fieldings, *Education for Ministry,* published by the Association for Clinical Pastoral Education, Dayton, Ohio, 1966, and Marvin Bower's book, *The Will to Manage,* McGraw Hill, 1966.

Discussion Suggestions

Discuss the way each person in a leadership position in your church is held accountable. How fair and thorough is the feedback each one receives? Is anyone getting hurt?

12

Manage Your Money

One test of our leadership of God's household is: Are we leading this band of disciples the way our "elder brother," Jesus Christ, led His disciple band? What would it mean for us to deal with "money matters" as He did?

Discuss Budgeting Seriously

Jesus never discussed budgeting in cool detachment like a smart business administrator reading "the bottom line." What people did with their money was always a life-or-death issue. He had grown up hearing His mother's lullaby "magnificat" song, which included the confidence that God would fill up the poor with good things and send the rich away empty. In His declaration of His own life call and vocation at Nazareth, He insisted that the supreme working of God's Holy Spirit in His life was going to be focused upon helping God's promised "year of jubilee" to happen. He said He felt anointed to preach the acceptable (jubilee) year of the Lord. He would not have been surprised to know that one of the supreme effects of Pentecost was that they had all things common, and that many sold properties in true jubilee fashion to meet the needs of the poor.

Jesus discussed budget by standing over the treasury and

commenting out loud about what people were giving, the widow giving her two mites, and the wealthy tipping God out of their abundance. Just try to do the same if you want to get demoted from your leadership role in the church!

Jesus discussed budget by overturning the tables of the money changers in the temple. His same Spirit discussed budget by smiting Ananias and Sapphira dead because they lied about their giving.

Consider Giving as an Act of Worship

Jesus seemed to suggest that one time to discuss budget and a disciple's giving might be right in the midst of bringing the gift to the altar. Even as the ushers are moving sedately down the aisle, and approaching the altar, a giver may remember that a "brother has ought against him." Christ urged that the lifting of the offering be halted while the guilty giver goes and is reconciled with the person he had cheated. Giving can only be completed, and the offering brought to the altar, after unethical methods of moneymaking have been dealt with. In like fashion Jesus only promised that salvation was coming to the house of Zacchaeus when the guilty rich man was ready to practice jubilee, and to make things right in money matters. Concerning the rich man who refused the property-selling jubilee spirit, Jesus portrayed him turning away sorrowful, tearing down barns so as to build bigger hoarding barns, and finally opening his eyes in hell. Financial unfaithfulness was always a desperately serious matter with Jesus.

Suggest Countersigning One Another's Personal Budgets

How can you, as congregational leaders, bring some of the same soul-searching intensity to the giving practices of your people, and to the budgeting practices of the church program? You might begin as leaders, by countersigning one another's budgets. As you start to spread out your own income and giving intention statements before a dyad partner, you would be setting an example of the transparent openness and mutual honesty about money matters which Christ and the apostles taught. In one congregation in which the elders taught and practiced the necessity of mutual admonition about faithful stewardship, up to 60 percent of the members of a large congregation became willing to countersign budgets with another couple from the same congregation. Needless to say, giving became alive and sacred, and it increased vastly.

Explore Zero-Based Budgeting

Some congregations practice "zero-based budgeting." By this method each program which requests church funds begins from scratch every year, justifies the program's continuance, and makes a fresh minimal estimate as to what the really crucial aspects of the program will cost. This gives the congregation a fresh chance to examine priorities. Too many budget planning committees merely accept the "status quo" uncritically, and try to treat all requests alike, granting them all a 5 percent increase, or penalizing all with a certain percentage of decrease. This is a "safe" but lazy approach.

If the entire congregation first dreams, prays, and plans ahead as to the program they feel God wants them to engage in, then they are better able to tie their budget building process to these plans. If each program committee hears what every other one has in mind for the year ahead, they are better able to "see-it-whole" and to decide what funds and resources they should request for the work of their own committee.

After bringing all of their program and budget proposals together, and having agreed together about the total budget and ways to raise the funds, each commission is better prepared to go back and do any final budget revision if this is needed.

Use Your Budget as a Focus for Family of God Self-Study

Some "experts" in congregational administration feel that the budget is where "the rubber hits the roads." Approving the budget can become the focus around which the congregation does its annual survey of needs and opportunities; tests them by theological priorities; develops its goals; projects its programs; surveys its resources of gifts, talents, money, and time; coordinates activities in order to avoid overlap; plans its fund raising and agrees upon its evaluation procedures. You may feel this is too cumbersome for your people, or too tedious and drawn out. In whatever way you do telescope them, these aspects all need your attention.

You know your people. You can respect their feelings, foibles, idiosyncrasies, and likes and dislikes. If quite a few literally hate-the-word-"budgeting," then don't use it. You can call it "our cheerful-giving-plan," our "giving intentions," "our faith giving proposals," or some other phrase your people invent with which they feel comfortable.

Include in the Budget a Call to Sacrifice

You will be wise to incorporate some call to consecration and sacrifice in the very way your budget is structured. Some people respond well to a "maintenance budget," plus a "missions budget," plus a "miracles budget." The "miracles budget" could include all of the devout hopes members have about causes they wish the congregation could give to "if we had the money." Members who challenge themselves and each other to sacrifical giving and to a simple lifestyle because of world needs are well on their way toward a whole new attitude about giving, budgeting, and fund raising. It's one of your tasks as congregational leaders to foster that attitude in every way you can.

If you fail as leaders to inspire to sacrificial giving, you should be aware that failure in stewardship poisons every other area of church life. Materialism is an idolatry which is desperately seductive and deadly. The love of money (more than the cause of Christ) is a root of all kinds of evil which will sprout out all through the church program. If your members succumb to the uncaring affluence and conspicuous consumption constantly advocated by mass media and shopping centers, the results in time and eternity will be tragic almost beyond description.

Provide for Above Budget Giving

If the larger denomination of which you are a part has "authorized" various church agencies (such as radio programs, homes, schools, camps, hospitals) to approach members for direct gifts, which usually do not go through your congregational budget, you should be clear what you as congregational leaders wish to do about it. You may be wise to approve certain fund drives and causes for above-budget giving. Your members will then be free to do their special interest giving through their local congregational treasurer. You will have a more complete picture of the total interests and giving of your people. Your church treasurer may protest about the mass of extra work this entails but you would be wise to secure secretarial assistance for the treasurer, rather than to lose touch with this vital aspect of your member's lives. Where people's treasure is, their heart will be also.

Keep Stressing Ministries Even More Than Money

In presenting your united "giving intentions" or budget to the congregation you will be wise to keep stressing the ministries your congregation feels called to engage in, and the programs of mission and service in which you desire to share. Only incidentally and in secondary emphasis notice the cost of each ministry. This keeps a positive and constructive tone in the meeting. If members must pare down the budget they do so regretfully, sorry that some ministries must be cut back.

If, on the contrary, you focus first and always upon money, upon inflation, upon spiraling costs, upon percentage of increase, and upon the "best bargains for our money," you secularize the tone of the meeting, bring out the worst shopping instincts of some persons, and reduce the session to competitive haggling with possibility of hurt feelings resulting.

Suggested Readings

Helpful books for further reading include one by Lyle Schaller, *Parish Planning,* Abingdon Press, 1971, and Charles F.

Kemp's *Pastoral Care with the Poor,* Abingdon Press, 1972, (O.P.).

Discussion Suggestions

Is your giving as a congregation so tactfully arranged that your people give with joy, sure that all is fair? How do you help to protect your people from unscrupulous fund raisers? How can you honor "the widow's mite" (the small gifts of the poor) and yet challenge members with large incomes to sacrificial giving?

13

Plan a Good Spiritual Diet

You should be as concerned for a balanced spiritual diet for the family of God as you are for your human families. This is basic. It undergirds all else that you do.

Remember God's Mighty Acts of Love

If you really see yourself as "God's people" redeemed and set apart by mighty acts of your Father God, then your whole year will orbit around what God has done and is doing to make you His people. The "church year" will be important to you. You will make much of God's act in sending His Son (Incarnation-Christmas); in overcoming evil with good (Good Friday and Passion Week); in His victory over the evil powers by the resurrection (Easter); in His mighty act in descending and showering back the enabling Holy-Spirit-given gifts for ministry (Ascension); and in His mighty act in sending His Holy Spirit to empower His people for world evangelism (Pentecost). You will observe these and other special days throughout the year.

Since you desire your congregation to feel God's call to be His obedient people in this year of our Lord, you will stress during the first six months of each year God's acts as Creator, Savior, Judge, Revealer, Leader, Redeemer, and Enabler. These

themes will be celebrated by God's mighty acts of Christmas
season on through Pentecost season, December through May.

Consider Your Acts of Loving Response

Your emphases the second half of the church year will be
upon the people's response. June through November is called
"Kingdom Tide" and celebrates in various ways God's people
praying and acting so that His kingdom may come and His will
be done on earth as it is done in heaven. Beginning with Father's
Day in June study faithfulness through our human families. In
July study obedience to God rather than man (while the world
stresses patriotism and the governmental call to war). In August
celebrate the Festival of Christ the King. He is King over his
family's leisure, vacation time, and spending.

In September over Labor Day study the challenge to bring
all vocation, daily work, and physical labor in line with God's
kingdom requirements. In October celebrate Worldwide Communion Sunday to help increase your awareness of the whole
church around the world who is living within the new covenant
of Christ's blood. In November celebrate Missions Week, renewing in your heart and minds Christ's challenge to go into all the
world with the good news of His saving love by calling out His
family, His people, His household. In November your people
can prepare again, through Advent themes, for the coming of
God's Son, and in the Thanksgiving season respond to all of
God's good gifts.

Omit the World's Secular Holidays

In stark contrast to the church year which compels the
interest of God's people year in and year out, you will be wise to
soft-pedal other celebrations which the secular world has instituted. These include those celebrations which accent narrow na-
tionalism, such as the birthdays of political leaders, independence
days, and patriot days. You will resist the temptation to shift the
meaning of Easter away from the resurrection and Christ to a
fertility-cult-emphasis upon springtime, fertility, and the sprout-

ing out of vegetation. You will avoid emphasizing other "special days" which detract from celebrations of God's mighty acts.

Plan a Diet Which Strengthens God's Family

In helping your nurture, worship, and fellowship commissions to plan ahead you can include also some denominational emphases and studies being suggested for the coming year. By the time you have written into your year's calendar the church year celebration outlined above, you will have the basic ingredients of the spiritual diet for the coming year.

Your vision and statesmenship will be supremely tested as you ask yourselves: Just what special emphases do we need in the coming year? What issues are looming on the horizon? What portents do we feel and see of crises which will be confronting our people and for which we should be strengthened in advance?

You will be a better "servant of the generation" if you prevent problems from becoming serious by strengthening your people in advance, rather than constantly dealing with crises after they have caught your people unprepared.

Do your people need to be fortified against materialism by a series on Christ's teaching about money? or against divorce by a series on covenantal love? or against spiritual coldness by a series on "prayers of the heart"? You are to see to it that they receive their "spiritual meat in due season."

Schedule Intergenerational Events

Your imagination will be tested by your ability to plan holistic, family of God, intergenerational learnings, in which your commissions cooperate to secure a united impact upon the intellect, emotions, and will. The school system with its graded and segregated classes, reliance upon rational transmission of facts, and grading upon the basis of factual recall will not be your model for helping a second-generation in the "household of God" to come to a first-generation faith. Interiorizing a personal faith calls for intergenerational decision-making, celebrations and festivals, and times of sharing the joys and sorrows which come to God's people. Your growing children have the best chance to understand the heritage of faith if they can watch their parents utilizing it to solve problems in line with Christ's call and teaching. In Israel, the children heard their grandparents shouting out their renewal of their covenant vows with God.

Develop Sermon Series as Needed

You will want to suggest to your pastor (or preacher-teacher of God's Word) certain expository sermon series that you feel are needed to balance the spiritual diet for the coming year. If the Sunday school curriculum focuses upon the Psalms, the expository sermon series may focus upon the Prophets. If your Sunday school studies are in the Gospels, the expository sermon series may well be drawn from the Epistles. By all means plan for continuity, developing great themes, so your people can achieve a depth of understanding. Avoid piecemeal, hit-or-miss, and hodgepodge sequences.

The person or persons you set apart, ordain, and charge to preach-teach the "whole counsel of God" from the Scriptures will need to serve as a kind of "theologian in residence." He or she will need help from the entire congregation to sense how to "bring out from God's treasures things new and old!"

Maintain Flexibility in Your Planning

Be sure to keep your plan flexible, ready to accommodate the new, the unexpected, and the concerns you could not have predicted. Christ made crucial use of interruptions, and your congregation should too. In spite of your best advance planning, "the wind bloweth where it listeth," the Spirit of God acts newly, and your congregation should be ready to respond. Your spiritual-diet-for-the year should not be so firmly set that you cannot respond to unforeseen events in the world, in your community, in your congregation, or in one of your commissions.

Suggested Readings

For those of you who wish to pursue this concern further,

you may find help in Howard A. Johnson's *Preaching the Christian Year,* Scribners, 1957 (O.P.) or the book by Lawrence O. Richard's *A New Face for the Church,* Zondervan, 1970.

Discussion Suggestions

First compile a list of the themes your congregation has studied in sermon series, Sunday school series, and otherwise during the past several years. Then list areas in which your people need strengthening for the years ahead. Now what themes and emphases should make up your spiritual diet? How will special emphases and celebrations already planned fit in?

14

Ordain the Preacher-Teacher-Equipper

As you lead God's household in the week-by-week experiences of their life together, you will find yourself relying always upon the spiritual gifts which the ascended Christ keeps giving to every member. Christ is the real Lord and "Head" of God's household, and He is the One who is "running" the church. Christ will send to members of your congregation the gifts they need if they are "gift-coveters," and if you help the congregation discern the gifts in every member and to call them into use. In light of all these realities, you may ask "Why do we need a 'pastor' " as some prefer to describe the task, or a "preacher-teacher" as still others prefer?

Expect Your Preacher-Teacher to Equip God's Family

Your household of God needs a pastor or a preacher-teacher of the Word to equip God's people for their work of ministering. The pastor is an "enabler" who assists members in their ministry. A pastoring person is one of the gifts the Holy Spirit desires to give to the church.

The pastor, or preacher-teacher, does his or her equipping for ministry supremely by opening the inner meaning of the Scriptures so that they can guide the lives of God's pilgrim people. It is as if God had preserved a family album of His ways of calling and leading His household, His people, His family for the period of several thousand years. These records (in the Bible) must be interpreted, taught, and applied in order to guide God's people in their pilgrimage. That is the task of the preacher-teacher-equipper.

You may protest, "Why not just rely upon every member's ability to teach the Scriptures?" This is precisely what is done for most of the nurture in the families of the congregation in the Sunday school and in the cluster or house church times of Bible study. Ordinary Christians can indeed read and apply the Scriptures with tremendous power and profit.

Ask That the Scriptures Be Opened in Their Depth

But the Apostle Paul was very wise when he insisted that a person "apt-to-teach" be charged to "give yourself to the preaching and teaching of the scriptures" (1 Timothy 4:13).

The truths in God's Family Album—the Bible—are embedded under several thousand years of cultural, linguistic, and interpretive accumulation of meanings. The truths of the Scripture are so deep and profound that they do not yield up their truest meanings, as the original hearers heard them, on a marginal time study basis. Mastery of the original languages and of word meanings in their original context is not given by charismatic gift, but only by dedicated study, patient exegesis, and persistent hard work. Only in this way can a preacher-teacher be a good householder, "bringing out treasures both new and old."

The household of God should set apart and charge a gifted person to "devote yourself wholly to the scriptures" (1 Timothy 4:15). This is because God has set the Scriptures (not the hierarchy or the sacrament) absolutely central in God's family.

Make Ordination a Charge to Preach-Teach the Scriptures

Ordination is the way God's household has chosen to set apart and to charge a member to "give yourself to the Word." It is a service of focused intercessory prayers, when members of the congregation do all that the power of prayer can do to call down God's blessings and power upon the life of one being set apart to preach-teach the Bible. Ordination should accent and emphasize the centrality and importance of the Scriptures in the life of the congregation. Ordination confers no special holiness, creates no hierarchy, and does not create a sacramental person whose presence defines the congregation.

Ordination can help the person thus charged to equip-with-the-Scriptures to say "no" to the one hundred and one tasks Protestant churches constantly heap upon their ordained leaders. The ordained person can insist that the congregation choose persons "full of the Holy Ghost to put over this business," even as the apostles did when they wisely decided to "give ourselves to the Word." Other persons, such as congregational administrator or chairperson, may be installed and commissioned appropriately. But you may be wise to limit ordination to the person set apart to exegete the Scriptrues as a long-term task.

Insist That the Pastor Avoid Overload

The pressures upon the ordained member will be intense. "Successful" churches on every side are served by pastors who "run" the church much as one would run a "Golden-Rule Country Club," or as one would run a "God-runs-my-business-corporation." Pastors in some churches chair church boards, supervise paid staff, oversee publicity, plan worship, administer the church budget, run fund-raising campaigns, instruct converts, visit the sick, mediate conflicts, counsel the troubled, perform marriages, officiate at funerals, represent the congregation to community agencies, make reports to denominational head-quarters, handle office correspondence, plan spiritual diet for the church, and then still try to find time to expound the Scriptures! No wonder they do not really preach-teach the Scriptures in their depth and power! No wonder that they wind up preaching bright little essays, assembling a few smart remarks upon a topic of current interest. And no wonder their congregations experience a famine for hearing the word of the Lord from Holy Scripture!

Fortunately for you, as leaders of the congregation, you can reach back into both Scriptures and into church history to warn against the focusing of all of this power and work upon the head of one person. The practice of asking (or allowing) a pastor to do everything for passive members who are thereby reduced almost to spectators is of fairly recent origin. Many creative attempts are being made to restore the preacher-teacher to more of a "theologian in residence," and by team leadership patterns to use the many gifts God's Spirit gives.

The pastor or preacher-teacher you ordain and charge to equip the ministering congregation from the Scriptures will see his or her main goal as that of producing a scripturally literate laity. This should lead to a congregation of active members who will utilize the truths of the Scriptures to guide their personal lives and their corporate lives together. Some preacher-teachers see their task as that of guiding a "Bible institute" in the congregation, offering special classes in Bible study, ethics, and current issues. They attempt to keep training their members in Bible study, evangelism, teaching, and social witness.

Ask the Pastor to Instruct New Believers

Almost all pastors feel that, as equippers of the congregation, they should instruct seekers and new believers or converts in the meaning and practice of the Christian life. This is indeed a crucial ministry, and a part of equipping every member for ministry. If new believers are to grasp the congregation's heritage of faith in its biblical, historical, and doctrinal depth, someone must plan and carry through vigorous studies and realistic dialogues around the crucial issues of faithful discipleship. The pastor should invest deeply in this process, and call upon gifted and mature members to help in seminars, debates, dialogues, and search groups which prepare new members for their baptismal vows.

Expect the Pastor to Relate the Bible to Current Issues

A preacher-teacher-equipper (or pastor) can offer carefully

thought through input on crucial issues. These may be assisted by the elders or congregational leaders. These presentations should be biblically grounded, historically researched, with specific suggestions for concrete application. Many mature members can test the pastor's exegesis and input, even though they could not actually do it themselves. These assigned issues and subjects may include problems triggered by crises in the congregation, needs in the community, or by personal problems of members. Issues like justice, war tax payment, divorce, affluence, abortion, strikes, poverty, racism, and homosexuality need such careful study and presentation.

Assign the Pastor to Serve on the Worship Commission

The pastor should be very active on the worship commission of the congregation. He or she should give much thought to spiritual diet. When the worship commission and leadership team have decided that the total spiritual diet calls for a study of certain biblical prophets, a series on the Psalms, an exposition of the Ten Commandments, a study of the Sermon on the Mount, or a study of eschatology, then the pastor can go to work in sustained, depth-level study. Ten to twenty hours of preparatory study may well lie behind each hour of teaching done in the church, or each expository sermon from the pulpit. Nothing else the pastor could do with his time dare be allowed to crowd out this kind of study.

Ask the Pastor to Model a Method of Bible Study

The pastor will actually be "modeling" an approach to the Scriptures through preaching and teaching done in the congregation. Members will sense the difference between marginal time study of the Scriptures, and the kind of richness and power which Scriptures can yield when they are wrestled with in their depth. In addition to teaching a method of Bible study, by the way he or she works through selected passages in public, the pastor may hold training sessions for teachers and congregational leaders. This would be a high priority upon the pastor's time.

Have the Pastor Assist in Visitation

The pastor should not be expected to do all of the visitation in the homes of members. As a true household of God, members will want to move in and out of one another's human homes rather freely. They will provide much of the total pastoral care of one another in this way. But the pastor should do some visitation and much crisis calling and counseling. Only then can he or she be reading the "Now-Testament" which God's Spirit is writing upon the fleshly tables of human hearts. Only when the pastor knows the real lives of people can he or she apply the Scriptures in their truest intent. If the pastor tries to be only a "theologian in residence," and only a biblical-scholar-teacher, the output will sound bookish, and ultimately irrelevant. The pastor must know and be known by the congregation in intimate reality. The pastor should know the profoundest concerns upon the hearts of members.

Have the Pastor Help Members Identify with Holy History

The pastor can from time to time exposit afresh the meaning of God's mighty acts. Each new generation must stand awed by God's acts of creation, in calling out His people Israel, in sending His living Word through His prophets, in sending His Son, in raising His Son from the dead, in sending His Spirit, and in purifying His household by His acts of judgment and mercy. No one else on earth will teach these truths unless the church does so, and no one else in the church should feel this obligation more keenly than does the person set apart to preach-teach God's Word.

Caution Your Pastor to Beware of Accumulating Power

If you are indeed accepting "the household of God" as your model to guide your shaping of congregational life and administration, then you should be keenly aware that this model has within it certain problems. The biblical model of a household is very patriarchal. There are assumptions that "a father" holds great power and authority. In most patriarchal household models the father is most closely linked to ancestor, tradition, lineage, and inherited wealth and power.

You can readily observe that many religious communes and devout intentional communities do actually adopt a patriarchal pattern. A few of their top leaders accumulate tremendous power, and some become a "beloved dictator." This is a real and desperate danger.

You will need to counteract these implied assumptions and tendencies vigorously. You will need to protect the pastor or ordained leader lest these authorities, assumptions, and attributions of power accumulate upon his or her head. The reality of a nonhierarchical brotherhood can easily be destroyed. A one-level membership could be lost. The good results which the woman's liberation movement has achieved could be lost, and a "sanctified male chauvinism" take over.

In your household of God you will need to stress "we are all sisters and brothers," "be not ye fathers," since "we have only one Father and He is in heaven." You will need to return again and again to the household passages of the Epistles in which radical mutual subordination is stressed, in which God makes the slave the moral leader, appeals more to the subordinant wife than to the male head, and assumes that young people can exhort elders (1 Timothy 5:1-2). You will need to keep stressing Christ's basin-seizing servanthood as the essence of leadership, redemptive love as the essence of headship, and the accumulation of power over others as the essence of the demonic.

The patriarchal pattern, so common in communes and Bruderhofs, is not the only pitfall, or the only bypath which can snare your preacher-teacher-pastor away from the task of equipping God's ministering people. Some preachers get a too-exalted conception of their own importance simply because "God called me to preach. . . . I must obey God rather than man." This can easily lead to arrogance and delusions.

Don't Let the Pastor Become the Expert Miracle Worker
Some preacher-teachers are led astray by their own oratorical

powers. They can "wow the back rows." After a while they assume that their human words always become God's living Word. Orators must beware of pride and of dogmatism.

If your preacher-teacher takes the time and the hard work (as he or she ought) to master the biblical languages, the history of Christian thought, the methods of counseling and pastoral care, and the dialogues around ethical issues, then he or she may be seduced into too much reliance upon "my training." Your servant may slowly but subtly come to feel like your master, because he or she has become a "professional," an "expert," or a "scholar." At the same time a remoteness and a coldness may develop.

Just as subtle as any of the above is that which snares "the miracle worker." When God grants charismatic powers and blessings and miracles, the preacher-teacher-pastor is often tempted to "play God." All too often a reflected glow from God's greatness and power begins to fall across the pastor, and his heart begins to be lifted up in pride. The pastor is on the way to ruin unless some humble prophet confronts and calls to repentance.

Those who believe in sacramental ordination tend to feel that they are set apart by the sacrament, empowered thereby to administer the sacraments, they have rights which are theirs alone; their presence defines the church, and therefore everyone else is a "layman." These are unfortunate assumptions, not borne out by the New Testament, and not helpful either to the church or the ordained person.

Help the Pastor Remain the Servant of the Congregation

Some authority does tend to go with the office, person, and the ministry of the pastor who faithfully preaches and teaches God's Word. The ultimate authority, of course, rests in God and His Son Jesus Christ, and His Spirit. The Scriptures partake of this authority inasmuch as they reveal, as nothing else does, the will and ways of the sovereign God. The pastor who expounds this authoritative Word wields some authority too. This happens whether or not the pastor wishes it to happen.

The call and charge of the church tends to localize and convey a sense of responsibility and authority to be an example to believers. Years of proven faithfulness adds weight to anyone's words, and this is true of the pastor too. But the operational, functional authority to bind-and-to-loose, to decide, to give or to withhold fellowship, to set standards, and to speak prophetically to the principalities and powers—this authority belongs to the church and not to one or more of her servant-leaders. Power always corrupts human beings, and ultimate power corrupts totally, so save your pastor from this peril. Structure your life so that your pastor is and remains the servant of the congregation. Do give your pastor honest feedback and a periodic review in great seriousness.

You can expect that some neo-Anabaptists will come forward attacking ordination itself, urging that the preaching-teaching of the Word be shared almost equally by laymen. They will amass many arguments why the congregation should not set apart, ordain, and support a preacher-teacher. You can salvage some wisdom from some of their arguments.

But you will notice that usually they are persons set apart and paid (as theologians, denominational executives, or whatever) so that they can give themselves to the Word, and to their study. You will wonder why they refuse the congregation's right to be served also by an "equipper with the Word." You will notice that they use their own education to turn around and attack the ideas of educated pastors serving congregations.

Even if opponents of an educated, ordained "preacher-teacher equipper with the Word" quote their New Testament to prove their points, remember that your congregation stands twenty centuries farther away from the Christ event, and trained exegetes to recover the meaning of the Christ are needed even more now than they were in New Testament times.

Suggested Readings

Parallel readings you may find helpful can be Carnegie S.

Calian's book *Today's Pastor in Tomorrow's World,* Hawthorn
Books, 1977, and George Sweazey's *Preaching the Good News,*
Prentice Hall, 1976.

Discussion Suggestions

Are you protecting your preacher-teacher from overload,
allowing for further mastery of the Scriptures and teaching their
truth? How might you better utilize your pastor's time and gifts
to equip the entire ministering congregation for their work?

15

Keep Members Informed

You should do something to help the members of God's household to "keep-in-touch." As leaders you may draw back, and protest that persons who deeply and truly do care about one another will see to it that they keep in touch. You may insist that the spontaneous calling of one another on the phone, stopping in to see one another, and writing loving letters to one another is better than any formal publicity you as church leaders could plan for or provide. You may argue that it is enough just to "trust the grapevine," and rely upon the "loving gossip." After all, people are very human; they love to spread the news, good or bad.

You are partly right. Our heavenly Father's little creatures, the birds and animals, have many loving calls to show where each one is and whether everything is all right. Anthropologists have traced among preliterate tribes many ways of sending signals.

You will be wise to rely upon your congregation's creative imagination to find ways to share news of one another's whereabouts and concerns. You can do a great deal just by reminding members that they really are members one of another, so that when one suffers all suffer, and when one joys all do need to rejoice together.

But you can call forward gifted members from your congregation to encourage the sharing of news. Some groups have a "hot-line" whereby all members receive calls by phone in a matter of minutes if something happens to one member. Other congregations establish "runners," who bear the news in person to shut-ins or others hard to reach.

Keep Recording the Family History

You may be wise to help members of your congregation to begin recording their history, a journal of God's leadings in their lives as His people. This testimony of God's dealings with them as His present-day-people could be called the "Now-Testament," and members could reread it reverently, contrasting and comparing it to the "Old Testament" and the "New Testament." By all means do more than to merely appoint a congregational "historian." This could result in a dry as dust list of facts.

Christ promised that sometimes a little child will lead. So find ways to let the childlike faith of the children in your midst to instruct all of you. Let their simple artlessness expose the mask-wearing adults fall into. Let their impulsive and honest prayers teach you how to pray in childlike faith. See that the innocent and profound questions they ask about life's meaning, death's finality, and God's availability are shared with the congregation.

You will be wise also to draw out and share with the congregation the mellow wisdom of your aged members. Even as godly elders felt obligated to create parables of wisdom to share their life's learnings with the oncoming generation, and God's people gathered them into a book of the Bible, so you should treasure the parables of wisdom which your older saints are able to share. But they will not likely write and share them unless you prod them lovingly and sincerely to do so.

Aged, as they enter a kind of second childhood, often begin to see life again with the sharp reactions of awe and wonder of a child. The trivial and ephemeral tend to fade away for aged saints, and they may be able to zero in on things which are durable and eternal. Your youth and young adults, constantly seduced by the falsities of advertising claims, desperately need such help.

Sometimes aged recover the ability to see the congregation as family. Some children really see everyone as an uncle, aunt, or cousin, as belonging to the family and so to be trusted as family. If any of your aged, as they regain elements of childlike spirit, are able to do this too, by all means find ways for them to help your congregation with their spirit and your wisdom.

If some of your aged are having sweet and sacred foretastes of heaven, feeling half in and half out of the body, find ways that their sacred insights are shared. If your aged have a deep gratitude because God does indeed find a way to make all things to work together for good to them who love Him and try to follow His purposes, help them to find a way to share their testimonies.

Discern and Utilize the Gifts of Your Creative Artists

Your congregation may be led to discern the gifts of your artists and call them to serve the church. You may commission for service several members proven in the artistic use of photography. Persons sensitive to "meaningful moments" or to "peak experiences" in the lives of your people may capture some of these meanings in pictures. As a congregation you may be assembling a family of God picture album much as good human families do. However, the person would need to be much more than a shutterbug with a flair for excitement. Photography done by a sensitive perceiver and a skilled artist-photographer could do for congregational life what some *National Geographic* photographers have done for beauties of nature.

Arrange for a Newsletter to Be Circulated

A congregational newsletter could become almost a "Diary of Anne Frank," or a "Journal of John Woolman," or a miniature "Acts of Modern Apostles," if you took it seriously, and if you assigned persons with both gift and calling to the task of assembling, interpreting, and editing the news. Probably a theologian, a historian, and a journalist from your congregation (or the nearest you have to these three talents) could make a good team to interpret what is happening to your people, between your people, and through them to the world. In many ways, the modern news media people are too given to bias and to sensationalization to provide good models for writers of congregational news.

People who are to share the news in its depth need to be keen observers of human nature, mature, and above bias or the inner need to be sensational. They need to be deeply spiritual in their view of life's sufferings and providential events, and highly articulate in order to share deep meanings in simple language. Persons who "share the news" need to have a keen sense of humor, yet have great tact to help persons to laugh *with* each other and not *at* each other. If someone is to fairly interpret events in the life of God's people, he or she must have great credibility. It might be good to have three or four viewpoints of the news just as Matthew, Mark, Luke, and John and give their view of original good news.

Charge Someone to Tell Your Story to the World

You need to be concerned, too, about how the good news of what God is doing in and through His household is interpreted to the outside world. You are not to "hide your light under a bushel." You are "a city set on a hill, which cannot be hid." You are to allow the light of God's loving work among you to shine. The watching world must be told what life can be like when people band themselves together to try to do God's will on earth.

You are justified to tell the world *who* has been and is involved, *what* has happened or been done, *why* it was so, *how* it came to pass, *when* it happened, and *where* it happened. Or, you can "advertise" a little (if you do it humbly) and announce to your neighbors and to the watching world what "feasts of good things" you are planning and to which they are invited. Few things will test your integrity as a people and your credibility before a watching world as will the way you present yourselves through your public relations and your publicity.

If you do as many modern religious hucksters do, and merely borrow much of the world's fanfare, the overuse of superlatives, the parading of cosmetic beauty, the promise of instant and easy pleasure—then you have betrayed God's people and His gospel. If your programs on television and your publicity through newspaper and radio merely call attention to the glamour of one of your leaders, or display affluence and conspicuous consumption like American advertising does—then you have not been faithful in relaying Christ's loving call to follow His way of the cross.

Keep Your Publicity Honest

It is important that your church publicity have deep intrinsic honesty. What your members do during their scattered lives all week, when they are busily "salting the earth" through their jobs—this must corroborate what you imply about God's presence and blessings upon you as His people. The promises you make about God's divine love which enables you to love one another and everyone must be borne out by the absence of divorce in the families of your congregation. What you say about God's righteousness and justice must be borne out by the fair deals your business people offer as they trade with the public. Your insistence that "Christ is the answer" must carry through in the counseling your members do in the agencies where they serve as therapists. What you say about "jubilee" and God's bias toward the poor must be borne out by the way landlords of your congregation treat their poor tenants.

If your preacher-teacher does preach over television, listeners should be able to turn off the sound track for a while, and be able to read sincere loving concern in his or her body language! All too often popular preachers thunder on and on about God's love with clenched fists and angry faces. This stark incongruity and phoniness is enough to nauseate discerning seekers after God's salvation.

If your congregation should dare to attempt the most difficult publicity of all, you might try to do as Hosea or Jeremiah did. You might try acting out the parables of Jesus. You will need infinite wisdom to know what the modern equivalent might be of Jeremiah's yoke, the prophet's sackcloth, of Christ's cleansing of the temple, or Paul's prayers said over handkerchiefs of the sick. The near-fatal temptation to pride and sensationalism is so obvious that you should pray long and pray hard. As God blesses your ministry with His miracle-working power, you all too soon are found doing your good works "to be seen of men." Then you already have your reward and the cause is hindered!

You will need all of the dove's harmlessness and the prophet's wisdom if you are to avoid two extremes. One is the answer of the Essenes or the pious monks who withdrew from the world into the inaccessible desert. You too will be mightily tempted to make of your Christianity a mere withdrawn, private affair, to become the quiet people of the land, to be careful to offend no one, and to limit yourselves to individual concerns of personal guilt and forgiveness.

The other extreme will be for you to "get on a lampstand" all the time, to go public, be prophetic, arouse consciousness about social wrongs, make pronouncements, protest, march, agitate, and crusade for a cause. You can "wreck your chariot in either ditch" very easily. Worst of all, different members of your congregation may well favor either one of the above extremes. For you to try Aristotle's "golden mean" or some least common denominator all of your people can agree upon may not seem very prophetic.

Contact the Editor of Your Local Newspaper

You will demonstrate quiet courage if you take initiatives to meet the editor of the local newspaper and the news reporters of the local television station. While meeting them face-to-face you can "be ready to give a reason for the hope that is in you," the "upside-down kingdom" you feel called by Christ to join, the "counterculture" lifestyle you feel is necessary for you if you are to be God's obedient people. Not many editors or news media people have enough sense of biblical history to recognize God's stranger-and-pilgrim people when they meet them.

Editors all too often have learned to expect that "church news" will be about an organ purchased, a pastor hired, a building paid for, a building unit dedicated, a social event held, a financial campaign climaxed, a tea held, a mortgage burned, or a social evening sponsored. They are accustomed to bulletins, reports, banners, letterheads, form letters, illuminated signs, or neon crosses. They expect to hear of hierarchy honored, money catered to, and prestige valued.

City editors may not know how to evaluate an upside-down kingdom in which the least are regarded as greatest, in which not many mighty are called, in which people share rather than selfishly consume, practice jubilee rather than accumulate wealth, forgive as they are forgiven, use the towel and basin rather than the sword, seek to serve rather than to dominate, love enemies, flatten hierarchies, and become as little children.

If the life of your people is as radically different as Christ calls His disciples to be, your editor friend may consider you a cult or freaks. He may pick up one of the ways you people dare to be different and quickly blow it out of proportion.

However, in spite of all of the above risks, you still ought to "meet the press." Your congregation has been called not only to tell the good news, but to actually be part of the good news.

Suggested Readings

Parallel reading may include such books as George W. Webber's *God's Colony in Man's World,* Abingdon, 1960 (O.P.), or Chester Pennington's *God Has a Communication Problem,* Hawthorn Books, 1976.

Discussion Suggestions

Examine carefully how your publicity interprets the life of your congregation. How well is every member kept informed? What has your congregation been telling the world, and how? Who in your congregation is recording its history?

16

Welcome New Members

Christ had promised that you as his brothers and sisters would not need to "compass land and sea to make proselytes" by high pressure evangelism tactics as the Pharisees were doing. Rather he assumed that if you would only be faithful in being the light (His light) to the world, many wistful seekers would come stumbling their way toward the light. If you only gave out His invitation to the "Marriage Supper," not all would make excuses, but some would come to the feast. If you demonstrated His life and power and loving call, not all would turn away sorrowful but some would want to follow the words of eternal life. If you only described a heavenly Father's boundless love, some prodigals would want to come home to Father's household. If you really felt you are a part of God's household feast, waiting to welcome prodigals home, the lonely and the lost would feel this in your joyful mood of celebration.

Christ always assumed that the evangelistic call was a call to follow as a disciple. It was not a call to say an intellectual "yes" to a code of verbal propositions. Evangelism involved repentance—to stop going away from the way He offered, and "faith" which kept saying, "Yes, Lord, yes and always yes" to each new step of commitment and following in obedience to His specific teachings and example.

Invite Persons to Know Your God as Their Heavenly Father

Jesus was supremely aware of His relationship with His Father, and He welcomed new followers by inviting them to be with Him, to get to know Him, to allow Him to serve their needs, and by sharing with them about the love of His heavenly Father. He discussed the issue they were interested in, and related that specific issue to their faith in Him as Savior, Messiah, and Lord. His disciples often heard Him praying to the Father.

These specific methods Jesus used are still your best methods. Your members will have many preferences about evangelism, and you will need to take their feelings seriously as you plan your evangelistic program. However, try to avoid merely selecting a "least common denominator."

Urge Your Members to Tell How They Were Led to Faith

You may be wise, in your attempt to unify your congregation around a program of evangelism, to ask each member to share, in a public session if possible, what method God's Spirit and people had used to lead them to faith in Christ and to following Him in the fellowship of His people. You can be sure that family nurture, friendship evangelism, faithful Sunday school teachers, and evangelistic preachers will get favorable mention. This procedure will help your people to continue to honor these methods in the congregation's present program of evangelism. In your openness to new methods of evangelism be careful not to ignore the methods God's Spirit has honored in the recent past.

Respect the Differing Viewpoints of Your Members

You should be prepared for very different reactions among your members to the methods currently in use by evangelicals and fundamentalists. If your congregation is "average," you will have some who value highly the methods of Campus Crusade with its "Four Spiritual Laws," and others who are completely "turned off" by this approach. You will have some who fully agree with mass evangelism and "crusade" methods, promotion, and appeals, and others who are almost angry at such evangelists because of what they fear happens to disillusioned seekers. You will likely have a few who wish to equate their social protests, their service projects, and their prophetic pronouncements with their evangelism, and others who feel that evangelism must be separated from all such efforts. You will be wise to move forward through the middle, respecting both sides but losing little time arguing with either extreme. It would be tragic beyond description if you allowed sincere differences in method to keep you from actually attempting evangelism.

Since you are leaders of the entire congregation you will want to honor any and every sincere effort (within reason) by which your members try to win persons to faith in Christ. Your motto may well be "by all means to save some." But do stress those methods which best fit a household inviting the potential sons and daughters of God to come home.

Try to Witness by Both Word and Deed

You will be wise to refuse the word vs. deed dichotomy, and urge that members try to give out one unified gospel whether by Word or by deed, whether by sermon or by service, whether by literature or by dialogue, whether by mass methods or personal approach. Encourage persons with differing approaches to seek to supplement each other, to support one another, to pray for each other, and to rejoice in one another's success if such befalls. Keep echoing the great themes of Scripture like "What doth the Lord require of thee, but to do justly, and to love mercy, and to walk humbly with thy God?" or "Come unto me, all ye that labour and are heavy laden, and I will give you rest."

Use Friendship Evangelism and Train Members for It

Friendship evangelism and fellowship evangelism may well be your main thrust in season and out of season. If you can provide some of the strongest leadership your congregation has (with the most Christlike personalities) and ask these members to lead out in a perennial program of friendship evangelism, this may be your best approach. Periodic training sessions should be provided for continuing members, and all new members should be asked to participate in the program.

Training sessions could include personal testimonies of efforts members are currently making in cultivating friendship with non-Christians. These progress reports could well be a part of every training session. Others in the training group could ask questions of those reporting, and in every way try to learn the lessons of tactful conversations, sensitive questioning, and loving listening.

Training sessions in friendship evangelism could well discuss ways to "move across" from the natural to the supernatural, from concerns of the day to concerns of human destiny, from the heart's hunger for love to the heart's need for divine love, from the human request to "give me a drink" to discuss the soul's thirst for "living water" which only the heavenly Father gives. Loving listening can be trained to hear the cry of the modern Nicodemus, the modern Samaritan woman, the modern Nathaniel, or the modern Zachaeus and to respond with some of the skill and tact of the Master. A careful study of the encounters of the Christ can still guide His people.

Your more timid members can help in friendship evangelism. Your household-of-God warmth, which meets your own needs for spiritual strength and growth, can be just what lonely, alienated, rootless persons are looking for. If you win members to Christ through the quiet miracle of human friendship infused with divine love, then that same fellowship group is already in action to provide the nurture the new believer needs. Your members, to whom God's Spirit has given the charismatic gift of hospitality so that they can love strangers into God's household, may find this the most rewarding ministry they ever do.

If some of your laymen and laywomen go evangelistically to their weekday professions as their strategy of redemptive penetration of society, you will be wise to give them your warm support. If some of your members try to represent Christ's love by their presence and spirit around the water fountain in the factory, you should try to rally the congregation's prayers behind

them for their daily witness and ministry. After all, you lay hands
on your members you send overseas as missionaries. Why not lay
hands upon and support with your prayers those members who
go to their factory, their office, or their neighbor with the same
sense of being sent by God's Spirit? Sometimes you might have
sessions in which all of your members who serve in the same
vocation or job could meet to share ways they are trying to
follow Christ in their work.

Practice Telling the Story of God's Saving Love in Jesus

Unless your members are very different from the "average"
you can expect that more than half feel tongue-tied, inept, blun-
dering, and unsure when they try to tell the good news of the
gospel to a friend. For some reason brilliant people falter, fervent
Christians become hesitant, and church leaders hold back when
they ought to speak. This problem will not be cured by challenging sermons, by buying evangelistic books for your library, or by
memorizing canned formulas. Too many will feel like "David
fighting with Saul's armor" if they try to use a method they read
about in a book. A few will feel that memorizing four spiritual
laws frees them to do personal evangelism, but likely more will
have problems with the trite formula.

You might try having sharing times when your members try to
tell the good news in their own words. They could hear one
another lovingly, help each other to "round out" the gospel story
as they tell it, and so by actual practice become articulate and
comfortable in their own personal way of telling the good news.
If your members' ability to tell the gospel story were emphasized,
stressed, urged, and commended as much as their ability to give
sacrifically, to attend faithfully, and to cooperate lovingly, then
you might little by little achieve an evangelizing congregation.

By All Means Keep Trying to Save Some

If mass evangelistic efforts come to your area, and you are
aware that many of your members are hesitant about either the
theology or methods embodied, what shall you do? You will be

wise to err on the side of cooperation rather than on the side of noncooperation and withdrawal. If you wait to cooperate in Christian service until you find ecumenical efforts in which you agree fully, you will wait a long time. Rather cooperate as far as you can, with as many of your people as feel comfortable, with a determination to be constructive. Try to upgrade the aspects of the program which you feel need this. Keep giving your testimony in humility and love. And keep on working away at evangelistic methods which you feel are your best approach all the while.

Keep Risking, Adventuring, and Innovating

Be prepared to keep risking, to keep adventuring, and to keep innovating. For a while you may secure the names of community newcomers from the Welcome Wagon or the water company and send your best visitors out two by two. For a period you may find church camping effective. For another period you may hold public services during the summer months in a local park. Another time you may follow up contacts made by your boy's or girl's club, Sunday school, vacation Bible school, or relief sale. Another time you may assist in a religious survey. Be willing always to begin at blind eyes, lame feet, or empty stomachs as Jesus did, and then to go on to point to a heavenly Father's love.

You may engage in prison ministries, in contacts through programs of tutoring, in work with migrants, in Book Rack maintenance, choir programs, discussion groups, Great Books Clubs, or any number of service and fellowship efforts in your area. In all of this it is crucial that Christ's imperative of His Great Commission remains your deepest motive, and that your methods are guided by tactful sensitivity, and energized by Holy Spirit power. Always you can seek to awaken some hunger that human persons have because of God's image within them. You may appeal to their desire to see meaning in life, to create, to enter covenants, to subdue the earth, to love, to plan, or to form a world-view. You can always share what Christ means to you.

Listen Lovingly to Those You Hope to Win to God's Family

Much of your evangelism will need to be done with a
"chastened mood." The world too easily senses the hypocrisy of
Christians "compassing land and sea to make proselytes," while
their own fellowship is shot through with pettiness, bickering,
anger, and lovelessness. Before God's evangelist goes out to
evangelize "this people of unclean lips," it is important to be crying out honestly, "Woe is me, my lips are unclean." Not only is
the unsaved world sleeping when God's midnight call to His
wedding feast is going out, but too often the church too is
partially asleep. Evangelism must include loving listening, and
the church must be prepared to listen humbly while the world
tells the church her failures first of all. After that the world may
be willing to hear the story of God's offered forgiveness.

Invite New Believers into a Face-to-Face Church Group

You will be wise to give special attention to the emotional
needs of husbands as you seek to assimilate new members. For
some reason they seem slower to give themselves to a group, to
trust it, and to feel it, than their wives do.

Encourage new members to invest deeply in a small group
of the congregation first, before they try to comprehend or feel
accepted by the whole congregation. Encourage new members to
submit themselves to a "gift discernment" process soon after they
join the church. Accepting a task, accepting responsibility, and
beginning to care for others soon builds loyalty to the church.
Being given an office in the church will feel hollow unless the
person first has learned to serve out of love.

Some new members will unite with your church because
they are seeking to discover their "roots." Maybe their
grandfather had been a member of a fellowship of the same
name. Maybe some say, "I attended Sunday school here when I
was a kid." These motives can serve for a little while, but the
person needs to feel family-of-God reality if he or she is to
continue coming.

The more diverse your new members are in social class,

ethnic backgrounds, and preferences as to piety, the more vigorous your small group life will need to be if "middle walls of partition" are to be broken down. As leaders, give special attention to singles and to persons won from a different background so that their specialness is honored.

Suggested Readings

Parallel readings might include books like Lyle E. Schaller's, *Assimilating New Members,* Abingdon Press, 1978, and the book by George E. Sweazey, *The Church as Evangelist,* Harper & Row, 1978.

Discussion Suggestions

Make a list of the 7 or 10 adults your congregation most recently won to Christ. Have one of your leadership team interview them, asking what method of evangelism won them. Why not deliberately vary your methods? What new methods might you try next year?

17

Provide for Space Needs

Accept the fact that God's family does need space in which to assemble. God's family dare not neglect the assembling of themselves together. They need to meet to exhort one another, and so much the more as they see the final day approaching. The Apostle Paul said that human parents and relatives who "refused to provide for their own have denied the faith and are worse than an infidel." You will not be good leaders if you refuse to face squarely the space needs of God's family.

When, as you always do in facing a problem, you look back through God's family album, the Scriptures, you find mixed messages about providing a building for the people of God. You find the passionate longing of the Psalmist David to build a house for God, and the lament of other prophets because some Israelites put other loyalties ahead of building God's temple. Alongside of this you find God's Son's warning that the temple was not really essential, but that worship in Spirit and truth was what really mattered. Paul picked up this refrain and stressed that the people are God's truest temple, and that the church can be satisfied to meet in spacious homes of members. Never once did either Jesus or the apostles lament the lack of a comfortable sanctuary, an aesthetic architecture, a prestigious building, or a holy place for God's family to gather. But neither did they urge ugliness, and deny the importance of an upper-room or a meeting place.

Expect That Some Will Want a Beautiful Building

Some of your finest, most sincere, and dedicated members are likely to feel that the God who created the sunset, the rose, and the tabernacle and temple must be a lover of lavish beauty. They feel that since the creating God takes the aesthetic needs of mankind so seriously, His people should do so too. They feel uneasy if their homes are more beautifully and comfortably arranged than is the house they build for the worship of God.

These members of your congregation will long for beauty and holiness to be brought together in worship, even as they are joined in heaven's worship. Beauty such as God ordered to be created in Solomon's temple helped Isaiah to sense God's majesty and transcendence. Such members feel a beautiful place of worship can help persons to look up, that beautiful symbols can speak God's praise in their own wordless way and can evoke deep emotions which belong in the adoration of God, and that beauty need not anesthetize the ethical concerns of the worshiper. For them the aesthetic and the ethical arousal belong together. They see both the cathedral with its symphony of symbols and the cantata with its symphony of sound as the most suitable vehicles of Christian devotion. For them it is only a Judas who cries "waste" when costly devotion (Mary's spikenard) is used up in worship.

Be reverent and understanding as you listen to those who speak of the power and sanctity of space. There is something profoundly reverent and right about their desire that all the symbols of the building, its use of light and darkness, its use of the vertical amidst the horizontal, and its blending of historical symbols with contemporary materials and ecology may point on and on to the God who is wholly other, yet dwells with His people. These worshipers are willing to address the God of all the earth, the One who inhabits eternity, as "Daddy, Abba." But first they want to feel prostrated, adoring, crying, "Hallowed be . . ." to the one encircled by the songs of the archangels, who dwells in the heaven of heavens.

And Some Will Want the Cheapest Space Obtainable

You will likely have some equally sincere members who feel they should worship in a storefront, warehouse, or home because world hunger is crying out for all available funds. They do believe that God wills to create beauty, and that worshipers should thank Him for all of the beauty He creates, but they feel that rich Christians should not create beautiful buildings while their fellowmen hunger for food. They do not opt for a poverty lifestyle because they regard it as a saving merit. They do not seek ugliness and tawdriness.

For them, to build a beautiful and expensive building would defy God's determination to liberate the oppressed poor, and to pull down the self-pampering comforts of the rich. They feel that they must be on the side of the poor, not only with their words, but in the way they refuse to spend money upon themselves. These members feel that no decent human family would spend lavishly for organs, air conditioning, and carpeting if some of the family were starving. They regard poor Christians around the world as siblings with them in God's family.

These members of your congregation will keep asking whether it is not possible for three or four congregations to rent and use one church building, fellowship hall, and kitchen. Why the lavish duplication of space which must be heated or cooled all week, only to have it standing idle three fourths of the time? At least they would want to give matching funds to inner-city and Third World churches before they agree to spend heavily for space for themselves.

Be sure you listen reverently to your members who feel quite sincerely that, to follow Christ, Christians should borrow an upper room to meet in, borrow homes as fellowship centers, borrow a mule to ride upon, and borrow a tomb in which to be buried. They have a valid point which our conspicuous-consumption, affluent, self-pampering times need to hear. They feel that the church might be a better mutually disciplined family if it refused to become so big. Then it would fit into available space too. Try to help all your people to hear these concerns.

Build with All Your People in Mind

When, after listening lovingly to one another, your people do decide to build, you will be wise to secure a good architect. You have many realities to symbolize. It is their job, their training, and their skill as architect to embody your faith in line, in form, in approach, in symbol, in use of materials, in design, and in the kind of beauty a building expresses. In addition, rightly used, they can usually save you more money than the fee they charge. An honorable architect worthy of his trust will try very hard to secure the beauty, the sense of mystery, the appeal to the transcendent that some of your people want and yet keep the simplicity, the frugality, the self-denial that other members want to see embodied.

But by all means do tell the architect the convictions of your people, history, faith, goals, emphases, and convictions. Describe the gatherings and activities your building is expected to facilitate. Too often building committees simply order up so much "churchly space" and the architect responds with something which speaks of his own ability to create novelty. If you hope to foster a believers' church faith, then beware of being sold the typical Protestant package of church architecture. Most modern Protestant buildings implicitly deny a believers' church faith.

It is important that you describe for your architect, in detail, which celebrations of the church year are especially important to you, what you want regarding ramps for wheelchairs, hearing aids for the hearing impaired, and other facilities important to those who you hope will use the building. Describe the history of your neighborhood, traffic patterns, and the total environment in which you are seeking to place your building.

To honor the convictions of members who plead for

frugality, you will be wise to plan for the multiple use of space. Design the kitchen area to also serve as classroom space, the sanctuary space to also serve for fellowship occasions, and the narthex space to double for library space. Your architect can suggest ways to use louvers, movable partitions, and movable symbols which can facilitate this multiple use of space. A custodian to rearrange furniture between the various uses will be much cheaper than the provision of separate space for each activity. Multiple uses of the same space saves real money in the original building cost, in heating, and in maintenance. Naturally no sloping floored sanctuary can be built if multiple use is to work. Some separate movable storage cabinets can hold the equipment small children need.

Secure Space Which Suggests a Spiritual "Home"

The access to the building should suggest a welcome. The sense of gatheredness should be such as is appropriate for a family. The central importance of the gathered meeting makes the term "meetinghouse" preferable to the term "sanctuary." Drapes and flowers at the windows, and provision for discussion groups can aid the homelike atmosphere.

Chairs (rather than bolted-down benches) which can be moved to fit the occasion seem most appropriate. A bright and homey atmosphere is important. Since it is important to see the expressions on one another's face, a dim religious light will not be suitable.

The Lord's table should be prominent. The breaking of bread is important in God's family. Its placement and easy access should suggest a welcome. It might well be the place the eye tends to come to rest—upon entering the building. You might symbolize the way in which the preaching of the Word arises out of your shared life and search if the pulpit or lectern to hold the opened Bible arose out of one end of the Lord's table.

One level brotherhood, without priestly hierarchy, can be suggested by a low pulpit. In keeping with the brotherly relationship of the preacher-teacher and the leaders of worship it is important that no "throne-chairs" be used behind the pulpit. It is suitable for the pulpit and Lord's table to be thrust far out into the midst of God's gathered people. It is also important that no rood-screen or partition separate the preacher-teacher-equipper from the people. A place for the elders to circle around the pulpit might be appropriate.

As in a good human family, so in God's family the person enjoys both freedom and belonging, both autonomy and community. In your spiritual home the individual should sometimes stand in solitary accountability before God and at other times should be immersed in an admonishing and deciding community. Always the proclamation of the Scriptures is correcting and guiding God's people. These realities should be symbolized in the way the pulpit is placed and the people are arranged for worship.

Secure Space Which Facilitates Your Activities

Since group singing is of tremendous importance, the acoustics should be such as to keep the sparkle in four-part congregational singing. If you deaden the acoustics by drapes and absorbent ceilings, you will achieve silent worship, but the life will be gone from your singing too.

Since baptisms, foot washings, weddings, funerals, and various celebrations of life's milestones are important in the family of God, your building should be arranged to facilitate the way you conduct these events. Explain these carefully to your architect, and be sure that the width of doors, aisles, and everything about the building is conducive to your activities.

If intergenerational education is more important to you than closely graded education, and if drama is to be an important educational method, your building should match these methods. If your building is to serve the neighborhood through a day-care program or some such ministry, your building should match these activities.

Because mutual admonition, mutual testimony, and sharing of concerns is important in your theology, your building should provide readily for these activities. Since choir members are drawn from the congregation, arise from it, and return to it in corporate worship, no separate choir loft seems required. If an empty cross is to be used to symbolize Christ's death and resurrection, it need not be spiked up against a wall, or carved there upon the furniture. If worshipers are to be following Christ in the way of the cross, it might appropriately be planted in the middle of the worship space, so that worshipers assemble beneath its wide stretched arms.

Keep Many Members Involved from Start to Finish

Be sure your members reach consensus as to the need for space, where to provide it, when it should be finished, what the shape should symbolize, the activities it should facilitate, and how much it may cost. How the building is to be financed while other budget needs are met undiminished is also a crucial question. Many meetings may be required to reach a consensus on all of these matters, but none dare be bypassed.

Even though the use of volunteer labor may not save a great deal of money, and although expert craftsmen sometimes dislike the presence of amateur volunteers, you may be wise to utilize volunteers just for the way it evokes and holds interest. Persons seem to care more about a project when some of their own sweat and toil is put into it. Also the fellowship of members while working together on the church building can be very valuable. In the modern urban congregation members have all too few occasions to do actual work together.

Your members who have felt so differently about the rightness of spending large sums of money upon a church building can grow together in a common agreement as they work together. Those who desire beauty can help to create it through honest use of materials carefully wrought, through stark simplicity, and through a symmetry and wholeness envisioned by the architect. Those who want frugality can help to achieve this by their volunteer labor. As their love for the family of God becomes incarnate in laboring together to build a house for that family, their work for God and their worship of God can be blended into one.

Congregation E. learned by bitter experience that it is very important to keep all the members informed and involved in the decisions as planning moves along. They would have been wiser to take an extra year to build than to leave one half of their members dissatisfied or feeling betrayed as it turned out in their case.

The building committee of congregation E. had looked at their growth curve, predicted how much space they would need in ten years, instructed their architect about multiple use, secured cost estimates, and laid out a plan for fund raising. They felt that their people were with them. Price estimates soared higher than they had hoped, and some influential congregational leaders, not on the committee, began to fear the large debt predicted. They indicated that they didn't trust the economy to remain stable, and that they feared being saddled with such high debt.

Finally the unrest exploded. In a congregational meeting the dissenters demanded that a smaller building be planned. The building committee resigned in despair. Much advance planning money which the church had given the architect was lost when he was dismissed. The program floundered for two years.

Even though another building committee was installed, another architect secured, a smaller building planned, yet people who had pledged liberally because they wanted a more adequate building felt betrayed as they were asked to pay for a building not to their liking. Quite a few members left the church.

Such a fiasco can throw a mood of discouragement over a congregation which may last for another ten years. Much of the tragedy could have been prevented if the building committee had kept in closer touch with all their people, and all of their feelings, at every stage.

Suggested Readings

Parallel readings regarding church buildings and meeting space needs may include such books as the one by Levi Miller (ed.), *The Meetinghouse of God's People,* Mennonite Publishing House, 1977, and one by James F. White, *Protestant Worship and Church Architecture,* Oxford University Press, 1964 (O.P.).

Discussion Suggestions

It seems clear that a congregation can be revived and renewed by the cooperation and consecration required to plan and to work together to produce a building to serve the coming generation. Why not send representatives from your congregation to find out how a congregation who carried it through successfully went about it? Begin planning for space needs before these needs become acute.

18

Manage Your Affairs Carefully

You can borrow some ideas from "management" theory as you seek to guide (or to manage) God's household. The Apostle Paul used the word which meant "a household manager" when he spoke of leading God's people.

Take a Positive Attitude Toward Administering-Managing

Your attitude toward administration dare not be one of "benign neglect." Neither can you get away with "laissez-faire" (just let it alone) leadership. Good congregational administration will not "just happen" because people are well intentioned. You will be well advised to give careful attention to methods of management. You may read some good books in the field and draw upon the knowledge some members of your congregation possess.

Unfortunately, there seem to be many more bad models and bad examples of congregational administration around than good ones. Even though few Christians seem to covet the charismatic gift of administration, or want to be administrators in the congregation, many have strong opinions about the way their church should be run.

Respect the Preferences of Your People

In selecting a way of organization for your people, you must take their expectancies and preferences into consideration. Some of their desires you must stand against too, at least partially so. Good management helps people to reach their fullest potential for their future.

Some of your members will want an administration like the "government," of "law and order," with good rules spelled out and carefully followed. They want detailed constitutions, and plenty of bylaws. They will want you to stress good traditions, to be slow about making innovations, and to declare yourself clearly on many issues. They may assign great power to you, because they sense that a powerful hierarchy can help to preserve the status quo. You may not agree with this segment of your congregation, but they are your people, you love them, and they must know that they are heard and their convictions respected. You may even have an "Archie Bunker type" or two to test God's grace in your life. Good management does insist upon clarity of understandings, clear definitions of terms, and openness about the values which lie beneath the group's rules. Good management is forthright about "the way we do things" and why. Good management establishes clear policies and procedures.

Help God's People Clarify Their Goals

You can be systematic about your search for what God will want you to do in your community. Beginning with the goals already given in the Scriptures, you can set out to make them contemporary for your congregation in measurable terms.

A survey of your congregation's history can help you to see what you are known for. You can survey afresh the people in your primary neighborhood: noticing mobile groups of persons, racial groupings, age-groupings, income levels, homeowner and rental groupings, and groups with special needs. You can study the growth patterns of your area.

Another survey can tabulate the churches and helping

agencies of the area, and who they are or are not serving. Then you can compare church growth with community growth, and church ministries with community need. Your survey might include the methods of outreach each church uses, the giving of each one, and their ministries in the community. Seek to learn who your own church has not been able to retain, and what class of people other churches tend to lose.

A deeper survey of the devotional habits, the giving habits, or the family strengthening habits of your people may be very revealing and useful. If you can, find out how many redemptive friendships your members maintain with non-Christians of the area. Out of this study draw conclusions as to your congregation's assets, weaknesses, priorities, relationships, and challenges.

All too often a congregation is exhausted by such a thorough self and community study. Your statesmanship as leaders will be tested by your ability to secure follow-through, to help your people to plan, and to take the next steps which the findings suggest.

Assimilate the Charismatic Members

Other members, just as sincere as the conservatives and probably even more vocal, may be the charismatics. Many of them greatly admire itinerant healers, exorcists, and strong leaders who wield charismatic power. They will want such leaders to be obeyed because God is speaking through them. The charismatics of your congregation are apt to want everything done by prophetic discernment. They may find ordinary structures and methods too inhibiting of the free following of God's Holy Spirit. Fresh revelations may cut across the consensus of the group.

All too often those who have spoken with tongues consider this to be an attestation of their spirituality. As a result they may be tempted to think of themselves as more advanced in the things of God. You will need great tact to keep noncharismatics from being turned off by their piety. Your statesmanship will be tested by whether you can appreciate the many good things the charis-

matics bring into the church, and whether you can keep them
and those opposed to their movement working together.

Use Good Management Methods

Good management helps diverse people to work together.
Some will favor a model more like that of a "therapy group."
Some of your members may have profited from "sensitivity labs"
with their confrontational honesty, or "therapy groups" with
their use of blunt feedback and exposure. They may want to lead
the congregation with these same methods.

You should be aware that methods which may "work" for
brief weekend meetings of like-minded persons who expect never
to see one another again may not be advisable for people who do
not want such methods used, and who will need to go on meeting
together for a long time to come. Good management does call
for awareness of resistance, respecting of feelings, giving fair
feedback, and being gentle in any application of pressure. Good
management commends any real growth, stresses the importance
of the person, and is as concerned about good inner process as
about outward progress. But the "therapy model" is not a good
one for congregational life.

Beware of Corporation Models

As a "householder" or manager of God's household, you
need to be aware that "corporation models" have crept unnoticed into church administration. Many are glad for this. They
want the church to run with one eye on the bottom line, the
losses, and the competitors; and one eye on successes, sales, the
growth curve, and the satisfied customers. They will want you to
follow the salesmanship model in proclaiming the gospel, the
competitive model in relating to other churches, and the marketing orientation as you decide whether a given church program
will "sell." But good management requires of you, as leaders of
the church, that you reexamine your charter, your reason for
existence, your history, and your mandate. You will need to
work against the corporation or business model of administra-

tion on many counts, including its hierarchical, line-and-staff, "know your boss" structures. As managers or householders for God salvage from the corporation model some of its insistence upon facts, avoidance of waste, awareness of the needs and desires of people, clear job description, and careful financial records.

Avoid the Country Club Model

As leaders of God's household you should be aware that elements of the "country club model" have infiltrated the church. There are unspoken assumptions that the church also exists as a high form of recreation. The church invites people to "forget the cares of your common life and come into our soothing atmosphere." "By soothing music, uplifting architecture, and positive thinking preachers we will help you to forget your troubles." "Come and join our club of the better people of the area. Here you will meet the successful people and these contacts will help you all week." "We have many forms of recreation, games, fun, parties, clubs, entertainments." "We are the icing on the cake." "We belong to the good life." "We offer a mood which will be good for your tired nerves."

As leaders of God's household you will need to protest and challenge most of the assumptions of the country club model. You may not insult people who hold such a view of the church but your prophetic honesty must speak out, albeit very kindly.

These management models (such as the corporation, the country club, or the therapy group) can be so powerful and pervasive that they stifle the household-of-God reality. A wrong organizational form can stultify the life of God's Spirit. This has happened repeatedly during the history of God's people and it could happen again today in your congregation.

Borrowing Unsuitable Models Can Harm the Church

For instance, God's people allowed themselves to borrow too many organizational forms from the Roman government, and the resulting church hierarchy gave the lie to the gospel and hindered the free working of God's Spirit. This happened slowly, imperceptibly, and likely felt right to the church at the time, but the results were tragic.

Later God's people borrowed the feudal patterns of medieval culture. The feudal kingdoms were paralleled by a feudal church. Again this probably seemed right but history shows that the pattern did not really fit God's household.

Still later, in the North American colonies, the church borrowed the democratic governmental structures of that era. The church copied ways of organization, representation, balancing powers, voting, mediating differences, taxation, election of leaders, and preserving freedoms. Today many assume that this democratic model is congruent with the life of God's household. They instinctively reject socialistic models in any way different from the ones they know. You will need careful biblical studies so that you can develop transcendent norms, by which you can evaluate your own inherited patterns and judge them wisely.

Consider the Tribal Extended Family Model

Some cultural analysts look away from the raw individualism of Western society and feel that the influences from tribal patterns are now needed by mankind. Many tribal patterns have good concepts such as the corporate personality, the collective mind, and the spirit of the group, which can help to foster strong community and group life. Members of the tribe tend to assume that the group is wiser than the individual, that reality flows from the group to the individual, and that the power of the group consensus should modify the individual opinion. Tribal people know how to keep in touch with their ancestors, how to value the transcendent, how to respect the wisdom of age, how to reach consensus, how to cherish community, how to sanctify the commonplace, how to value the extended family, and how to give members emotional security. These may be strengths you can draw upon so that genuine household-of-God congregational life can thrive. Perhaps church leaders from Africa and the Third World can be used of God to point the way toward new patterns of congregational vitality and reality.

Suggested Readings

Parallel readings may include books like the one by James C. Fenhagen, *Mutual Ministry,* Seabury Press, 1977, and one by Elizabeth O'Conner, *The New Community,* Harper & Row, 1976.

Discussion Suggestions

How would you need to change your administration and management of your congregational life for it to function more fully as a family? Examine all of your leadership methods to see whether they are suited to your faith, and whether your methods fit your people. Identify any of your administrative methods which fit a corporation model better than "God's household."

19

Solve Your Conflicts

Our Father God has very high ideals for His family, especially as to the way they resolve conflicts. Only those who actively work to create or make peace are truly His children. He doesn't only plan an eternity and a heaven in which peace reigns, and all conflicts are resolved, but He seeks to give His "shalom" (His reign of peace) to all who will obey Him, here and now. He has given to His family the ministry of reconciling which He began in His Son Jesus Christ.

Learn from Abel as a Hero-of-Faith

God's Word makes brother-hating equal to murder, and uses weak persons like Abel (whose very name meant weakness, unable, or a puff of breath) as heroes of the faith. Abel resolved conflict by trusting, by making himself vulnerable, by going along out in the field to talk over the damage his livestock had done to his brother Cain's crops. Then he offered to keep talking in the spirit of worship as he and Cain brought their gifts to the altar (Genesis 4:2-4). He offered his economics to God. He was ready to practice radical subordination with his brother Cain. Even though his brother was not willing to be reconciled while bringing his gifts to the altar, and murdered him in cold blood,

Abel's way is still viewed as a model (Hebrews 11:4). Christ cited Abel's way as He urged His disciples to be reconciled as they together approach God, in worship. They are to leave their gifts at the altar until they are really reconciled. You might be wise to keep teaching this as the only honest way to bring an offering during worship.

You will be wise to keep teaching, preaching, and modeling Abel's way of vulnerability and openness in all the conflict resolution needed in your congregation. Abel overcame Cain's evil with good, even though, like Christ, he lost his life in the process. Abel's blood still speaks to us and to all of God's children. God does not guarantee that enemy loving will always succeed as the world describes success.

And from Others of God's Family in the Past

In addition to Abel's heroic trustfulness and defenselessness, you can observe and keep teaching many other principles and methods of conflict resolution from the lives of God's family in earlier eras. You can point to Isaac's second-mile patience and altruism when angry neighbors stole his wells. You can study Joseph's nonresisting love for his unfair and unkind brothers. You can trace Daniel's endurance of slander and hate and the ultimate triumph of his way of love.

You can be inspired as you study Abraham's resolution of the conflict between his herdsmen and those of his nephew Lot. You can be sobered as you study the methods of Cain, Lamech, Joseph's brothers, Jacob, Jezebel, Nebuchadnezzar, Pharaoh, and King Saul. Alongside of these you can examine the methods of Mordecai, Queen Esther, Jeremiah, John the Baptist, Jesus, Stephen, and the Apostle Paul.

Work at Conflict Resolution

In spite of God's will that His sons and daughters be peacemakers, you will keep finding to your chagrin that church members get into conflicts rather readily. This is partly because sheer closeness causes conflict, and partly because issues encountered in the church are regarded as very important. In the church the ideals people hold are very high. Members all too readily see their own preference as God's will, and any other option as sin. Often a Scripture verse or two, used as a proof text, allows them to feel that they are really "defending the faith" when they hold out for their own opinion.

Conflict comes all too easily in the church because some clothe their very human power-hungers with divine sanction. They feel "called of God" to lead out. To make matters worse they may deny their real angers and pretend a saccharine sweetness which they do not really feel because they know they ought to love one another. Conflict may be pushed under the table, and may be thinly disguised beneath doctrinal arguments. A person unsure of his or her worth may feel a great need to champion a worthy cause while one with slumbering guilt may seek to atone by sacrificing self for others.

In other social groupings such as a labor union or the parent-teachers meeting of the school some Christians may be able to speak out and to work through some conflicts calmly. But within the church they find it hard to own up to their angers, to speak clearly about their convictions, to admit prejudices, to reassert caring, to risk trust, and to forgive when the case is closed.

The present conflict may awaken unresolved conflicts from childhood, or reactions from an earlier hassle may be transferred to this conflict. If members were hurt too many times earlier when they risked closeness and vulnerability, it will be harder for them to risk trusting now. If persons were rejected when they received poor grades in school, they may have trouble admitting any failure now. If members can't live with their own shortcomings, they may have a hard time living with them when they see them in others.

Restudy Christ's Instructions in Matthew 18

You will likely find (if you haven't already) that a lot of the conflicts which tend to go unresolved in the congregation are cases in which one member holds a grudge or a hurting memory against another, and the two persons simply can't or don't talk about it. A careful study of Christ's teachings in Matthew 18 about how to intervene, mediate, and reconcile an alienated brother might well be repeated every few years in your congregation. One year you might have several exegetical-expository sermons on the passage, and another year an intergenerational dialogue interspersed with dramas and life situation studies and case histories.

Be sure that your studies of Matthew 18 go deeper than mere surface observations—that a reconciler must initiate, must respect the grieved person's freedom by going to him alone, must respect the person's freedom and right to say "no" to you (be to you a heathen person if he chooses), and must accept a third party's report so that every word is tested and factually established, etc., etc. All of these are important skills and attitudes in resolving a conflict. But Jesus had just finished listing some very deeply probing essentials before He promised "if he is hearing you (implying all these realities) you are already gaining your brother" (Matthew 18:15).

Our secular world has developed a vast system for conflict resolution, with lawyers, judges, and juries gathering adversaries to face one another. As God's children you can observe their methods which include: getting hard facts rather than hearsay and gossip, considering one thing at a time, securing an unemotionalized and fair climate, submitting the case to neutral and impartial arbitrators, and insisting upon fair payment of damages. All of these are minimal aspects of fair play which you will want to keep in mind. But as God's children you will want to go much deeper.

Examine Your Own Attitudes

Christ promised that you will be gaining your offended brother only if he is hearing subverbally some very profound attitudes dwelling deeply in your own heart. Your offended brother needs to be hearing that you really consider yourself a

great debtor, a bigger sinner than he is. You know you owed 10,
000 talents whereas he owed only 100 denarii. (Matthew 18:24
and 28). You can't reconcile if you feel like a superior Pharisee.

Your offended brother needs to sense that you know that
you can't be forgiven at all before God unless you come to him
offering forgiveness in advance (Matthew 18:35). Your whole
existence as a Christian is in the balance and you know it. God's
forgiveness simply cannot keep flowing into your life unless you
allow it to flow on through you to your alienated brother. You
do not come demanding justice, but offering mercy in a similar
way as God does.

Your grieved brother needs to feel that your offer of forgiveness is uncalculating, uncounted, untabulated, and offered un-
grudgingly. You can't be asking, even in the secret recesses of
your heart, "Lord, how often must I forgive this guy?" (Matthew
18:21). The world in the secular courts may notice how often the
offenses have been repeated, but Christ wants His brothers and
sisters to continue to treat one another as first offenders!

Christ probed still more deeply and warned that for you to
be a reconciler you need to go seeking out your alienated brother
with some of the same infinite compassion with which the
shepherd leaves his 90 and nine and goes to seek the one stray
sheep. Have you really left your 99, your group who stands with
you in squad formation, and are you willing to move on out to
stand beside and identify with the straying brother? Can you be
with him on his lonely spot of turf? Can you feel what he feels?
Can you identify so deeply that he senses that you know how he
feels?

Christ hinted that while you are telling your alienated
brother his faults he is hearing whether you stand in humble awe
before the cosmic effects of what you are doing. While you are
bawling out a "little one" His guardian angel is even then
"beholding the face of our heavenly Father" (Matthew 18:10).
God and the angels are talking about your attitudes and loving
skill as you tell a "little one" or an offended brother his faults. If
your alienated brother is hearing that you sense in humble awe

the sacredness of what you are doing, and if you are deeply concerned not to offend him in the midst of his littleness, then you are gaining even as you are talking to him.

Deal with Sin in Your Own Life

Christ implied that even while your brother is hearing you telling him about his faults at a much deeper level he is also hearing whether you know from costly suffering how to get victory over your own fleshly lusts. Have you ever "cut off a hand or foot" rather than to continue in a sin? This is Christ's way of asking whether you have ever come to a life-or-death, now-or-never determination to quit a given sin. Do you really know the cost which sometimes must be paid to break a deeply engrained sinful habit? (Matthew 18:7-9). Your brother can hear you talking to him about a victory over sin in his life, if he senses that you are a person of self-discipline, and if you know what it has cost you to achieve holy living.

Christ implied also that your offended brother also hears whether you would prefer to shut up and quit talking rather than to go on talking, if what you are saying is not truly helping him. Christ inferred that if your talking is only driving your little-one-brother into deeper sin, you should want your voice to be silenced by drowning with a millstone around your neck! Christ asked for a "blot me out" kind of caring. He insisted that you should sincerely feel that you would rather die yourself than to drive your little-one-brother away (Matthew 18:5-6).

Christ made brother-winning, peacemaking, and the reconciling of conflict absolutely central among His children. But He insisted that this awesome and sacred process must be undertaken with childlike simplicity. You will need a child's readiness to keep responding to Christ's call. You will need a child's readiness to forgive and forget and to make up (Matthew 18:1-4).

For Public Conflict-Resolution Consider Acts 15

For your public sessions of conflict resolution, when members have polarized themselves into two positions, you may well study repeatedly and deeply the conflict resolution methods of the Jerusalem conference (Acts 15). As you trace the following principles and methods, stop and discuss what it would mean to utilize them in a conflict current among your people.

Notice carefully those issues around which disagreement and conflict emerged repeatedly (Acts 15:1, 2). Circumcision was such an issue in the early church. What are your issues? Try to keep them from becoming personal so that individuals do not feel they are being attacked as persons.

You will be wise to see the conflict within the larger mission of evangelism and church growth to which you are called. The apostles were busily commending some workers to God's grace as they sent them out in evangelism. Now these workers were reporting back what God had wrought (Acts 14:24-26). Ask how centrally the issues are related to evangelism and church growth. If it is peripheral you may take the issue with lesser urgency. If it is vital and central you have a first-magnitude problem. Relate the conflict to a basic congregational goal and help everyone see how the issue is related to your ability to reach that goal.

Try to get the problem considered as near to its source or "home base" as possible. The persons insisting on circumcision came from Jerusalem, so their home church at Jerusalem had to deal with them. Even missionaries should be accountable to their home or sending congregations. You can't solve conflicts among tourists or transients very well. What would it mean for you to trace your problem back to its "home?"

The Jerusalem conference illustrated another valid principle of conflict resolution. They selected representatives who knew something about the problem. It is not helpful to merely pool a lot of innocence or ignorance. To solve a conflict you need people concerned about the problem and informed about its history. The representatives need to know that the group has chosen them and has confidence in their ability and integrity. They are trusted to isolate the issue, consider its aspects one at a time in logical order, and work through to a solution which is fair to all.

The representatives went to their conflict resolution session in a joyful mood, and not in a grim and angry spirit. En route to Jerusalem they kept talking about the conversion of the Gentiles and spreading great joy as they went (Acts 15:3). Every church conflict should be considered alongside of the victories, joys, and the hopeful aspects of the total church program. Your issue will not get fair treatment if delegates go to discuss it in a spirit of despair or pessimism.

You may find that a warm-up period in which participants first share experiences of joy will prepare them to trust one another and to sense that potential oneness. Then when they shift to discuss their area of conflict they will likely do a better job.

In conflict resolution it is tactful to give the minority the first voice. The agitators who wanted Gentile evangelism to be rolled back until it made converts into Jewish proselytes spoke first. There was much debate, according to Acts 15:7. This is important in resolving church conflict. People must know they have been heard. A denial of real feelings will not do. A hurried vote which presses the minority down in defeat will not resolve the conflict at all. The conflict will reappear under other guises.

Announce Your Own Changes of Mind

In resolving a conflict it is supremely important that the opinion formers, the weighty brothers, or the central advocates of one position or another should humbly and honestly announce publicly how their mind has been changing. Very often, if these announced changes of mind all point in one direction, that is where the group consensus will emerge. Peter, who changed his mind after his vision from heaven, announced how his mind had changed (Acts 15:6-11). Then Paul, who had changed his own mind after his Damascus road encounter, told of the blessings he had been observing (Acts 15:12). Finally James told how he had changed his mind about the interpretation of an old promise in the Scriptures. He now sensed that the ruins of David would be rebuilt, not as Israel achieved Pharisaical purity and obedience to the law, but as Gentiles were brought into a new Israel by God's saving grace through Jesus (Acts 15:16-18).

If your members are to become willing to announce how their mind has been changing, they will need basic humility about their own omniscience and openness to believe that the group's wisdom may be better than their solitary wisdom. You may need to model this yourselves, as congregational leaders, before it begins to happen regularly during conflict resolution sessions. When it does begin to happen a whole new era of congregational decision making may open for you. Pride of opinion, which refuses to admit a change of mind, is one of the most subtle, pervasive, and pernicious forms of pride. The ability to accept the group's wisdom and admonition and to be changed by it is radical mutual subordination.

In the conflict resolution at Jerusalem, the group alternated periods of silence and reflection with periods of intense discussion (Acts 15:12 ff.). This is a useful principle. Emotions can cool, participants can search their own hearts in silence before God, and all can sense whether it is profitable to go on and on now. In some cases a conflict resolution session needs a recess more than additional new input or debate. Try to keep the conflict unemotional, channeled, and focused, and avoid having it become diffused over other areas of concern or lost because participants have become confused. Times for incubation and silent reflection can help a group to resolve its conflicts with less residual hurts.

A conflict is not resolved until someone comes forward with a clear proposal. The proposal is given for testing by the group, to see whether it does indeed represent a consensus which has been reached implicitly. The proposal James articulated was a wise one in that it asked for minimal rather than maximal agreements. The proposal was limited to what the present group had authority to say. It spoke for the present group. It did not attack anyone else's position. It had a conciliatory tone. It affirmed the sincerity of those who read Moses and who had wanted to require circumcision. It included cautions that "the losers" of the session wanted (Acts 15:6-21).

Finally, conflict resolution is not complete until the new

consensus is admitted to be a new leading by God's Holy Spirit. "It seemed good to the Holy Spirit and to us" (Acts 15:23-29). The new consensus should also be put into writing, into clear and unambiguous prose, and sent to all those concerned. It is important that the decision be spread in the spirit of "joyous exhortation" (Acts 15:31). Judas and Silas helped Paul and Barnabas to carry the consensus report. It is best that the persons whose opinion won out in the conflict resolution sessions should not carry the reports alone.

Resolve Conflicts Behind the Scenes

However, not all conflicts need to be dealt with openly and head-on. Two of the very common ones—the presence of a charismatic small group within the church and the family-in-power holding too many key church offices—can be dealt with quietly, gently, tactfully, with much of the resolution going on behind the scenes. As mediators you can talk one-to-one to suggest solutions. You can elicit the gifts and show that you appreciate the party out of power. You can deflect gossip about the charismatic group, which is regarded by some as a clique. You can show that you appreciate everyone equally, have no favorites, and are especially sensitive to persons who for one reason or another feel out of it. You can monitor your own feelings by the love chapter (1 Corinthians 13) and by the fruits of the Spirit (Galatians 5). If just ten or twelve others silently join you in those approaches, the conflict will lessen.

Study Paul's Advice to a Mediator-Yokefellow

The Apostle Paul asked a "yokefellow" to attempt some conflict resolution between Euodia and Syntyche in the congregation at Philippi (Philippians 4:1-8). Much of Christ's teachings in Matthew 18 and of the wisdom of the conflict resolution sessions of Acts 15 seems to be in Paul's mind as he instructs this yokefellow to serve as a mediator in a conflict in the family of God. Paul suggests both behind-the-scenes and overt actions.

In mediating a conflict, Paul urged that the members temporarily in conflict should not be scolded as if they were sinners, but were to be approached with deep respect. Paul reminded the yokefellow mediator that the persons now in conflict were his honored co-workers, and that their names are in the Lamb's book of life. Some conflict should be expected, regarded as normal, and almost welcomed as the forerunner of new insight and growth.

Paul stressed again that keeping a mood of joy and optimism was supremely important. He stressed the same truth that Christ taught in Matthew 18—that conflict resolution mediates His immediacy. Conflict resolution brings theophany. When you are mediating a conflict "the Lord is at hand." The living Christ intervenes also when you intervene to reconcile conflicted members of God's family. He warns against a mood of anxiety. He urges the mood of thankful prayer. He encourages the mediator yokefellow to be claiming God's shalom, believing that God is even now establishing His reign of peace. Reconciliation as an act of God's power and grace is happening (Philippians 4:7).

When God operates in His renewing power, opponents need not merely withdraw, or allow themselves to compromise their convictions, or win over one another. God's Spirit often enables a new way which incorporates something better than either opponent foresaw. God can help opponents to find a highest common denominator rather than for both to be forced to settle for a lowest common denominator. You expect this because God has promised to be "at hand."

Your Attitude of Forbearance Is Absolutely Crucial

Paul lifted up several more absolute essentials for a mediator, a resolver of conflict, or a yokefellow. In verse 5 he urges, "Let all men know your forbearance." As a mediator you need a reputation for patience, fairness, reasonableness, and for the ability to see both sides of any issue. You need to develop those qualities over the long pull, and then when a mediator-reconciler is needed, both of the estranged parties know that you are that kind of person. You might be wise to institute a few training sessions for mediators so that many in your congregation are known for their forbearance.

As his final instruction to yokefellow mediators, or conflict resolvers, Paul urged a persistent mind-set to see the good, to notice the positive, and to be aware of the hopeful. He insisted that the mediator set his or her mind persistently toward evidence that is true, honorable, just, pure, lovely, gracious, excellent, and worthy of praise. In times of conflict your slumbering angers tend to become aroused and you tend to see in others the unlovely, the untrue, the unjust, and the dishonorable.

As a Christian mediator-yokefellow your mind needs to operate almost opposite from that of a news reporter for a secular newspaper. Reporters tend not to notice and report the honest citizens, but if one person robs a bank it gets noticed carefully. Reporters seldom write up the happy marriage but only the divorce. They seldom write columns about the pure woman, but the impure one gets the attention. People living worthy of praise are not cited as often as the ones who are to be blamed. As a Christian mediator you are to focus upon the good in people.

As God's family you are to be a "counter culture." In the way you act as peacemakers and conflict resolvers, your lifestyle will be very different from the culture around you.

Keep Learning What You Can from Secular Mediators

In addition to the many principles to guide effective conflict resolution which you can draw from your study of the Scriptures, you will be well advised to keep reading from the abundant literature which social scientists are producing on the subject. A few of the many available will be listed at the end of the chapter.

To resolve conflict, mediators need to establish a commonality of meaning, to help persons to move beyond feelings of apathy and powerlessness, to facilitate careful listening, and to encourage patience. When you are serving as a reconciler you will want to observe carefully whether opponents are seeing the same data or experience from different but allowable perspectives. Some mediators have been known to ask opponents to switch sides for a while and argue the issue from their opponents' point of view. This convinces everyone that all involved do see both sides of the issue.

In resolving conflict you keep asking yourself and the opponents—whose problem is this? You may call upon each one to trace its history and present importance. You find out what has already been tried. You observe the degree of trust or distrust which is present. You are alert for exaggerations. You call a halt when either party becomes unfair. Call for more facts when these are needed, keeping yourself unbiased and neutral all the while.

In your role as mediator you may summarize the progress made and claim areas of common agreement. You applaud new sight and insight. You applaud new consensus. You affirm the person who has the humility and courage to ask forgiveness when that is called for. You try to be sensitive to issues which have sacred meaning to either party and you help the opponents to respect one another's conscience. You point out basic agreements where these truly exist. You celebrate any harmony which is emerging, and contrast it with the chaos and confusion which has been overcome. You keep implying that the former opponents are people of good will who can and will come to agreement if given time and understanding.

Suggested Readings

Additional readings in conflict resolution might include Alan C. Filley, *Interpersonal Conflict Resolution,* Scott Foresman, 1975; and Michael R. Tucker, *The Church That Dared to Change,* Tyndale, 1975

Discussion Suggestions

Review together the last several conflicts your congregation faced and trace how these conflicts were resolved. Notice whether your members tend to "go to law" against one another. Is Matthew 18 being practiced? What issues need arbitration, mediation, and working through right now? What next steps should you initiate?

20

Test Your Methods and Motives

Following are some suggestions drawn from the literature on leadership and management. Why not relate each one to your own actual performance? Grade yourself with a short descriptive sentence after each of the following paragraphs. Then discuss the results in your leadership team.

Try to coordinate the activities of others so they can better achieve their chosen goals. You can be serving Christ as you help God's children to cooperate. You can make participation possible and pleasant for people. You can try to humanize relationships where persons need to interact so that they do not unknowingly dehumanize one another or make anyone feel like a nobody.

Keep holding up high standards. Your leadership will be supremely tested as to the way you can relate these standards to the present situation. Your people must feel that standards are realistic. A good leader must be able not only to say "this is the way we do things," but "why we do as we do." This is realistic for the actual situation we are facing.

Help people to go from their standards to some specific operational plans. If you constantly proclaim your high standards, but cannot show how they are reflected in realistic and reachable operational plans, your people will feel let down. Your exalted statements that you feel called to evangelize your private world or neighborhood will not ring true unless you have helped to lead your people to assemble a responsibility list, the names of specific persons in the area, in your families, in your places of employment whom you sincerely intend to relate to in winning love.

Encourage Good Cooperation

Build upon strengths. You can do this if you help people with complementary gifts to find and support one another. The person with gifts in art will be backed up by the person with gifts in creative writing as they prepare congregational mailing to shut-ins.

Scrutinize the policies and procedures which actually function. Help to smooth out the flow of things. Often people are not clear to whom they are responsible, and to whom they owe reports and when. They often are not sure how much should be written, how much should be oral, and at what points their way of doing things is annoying to a co-worker. You brood over the family, facilitating their good intentions to do things together in a mutually enriching way.

Be concerned that all available resources are being deployed to reach the group's goals. You enlist the bench warmers, call forward the timid, and try to enhearten the discouraged. A part of your leader's task in this will be to distribute the necessary information from time to time. Everyone needs to feel on-board, sharing in the important secrets and crucial information. Be sure you know who is doing this in your congregation.

When decisions need to be made by the groups be sure that basic ethical principles are in focus, that important values are being respected, and that all have the necessary data so that they can help to make a "fact-rounded decision."

Maintain a Gentle Urgency

Keep inviting feedback. You need to be mature enough to

allow your partial failures to be exposed. If you provide usable tools for persons to evaluate your performance, you build trust that you really do value the opinions of other people. If and as you incorporate the feedback you get into creative improvements, you are modeling one of the most important principles of servant-leadership.

Keep a gentle pressure and a quiet urgency for the group to keep moving forward. All too often groups begin to "eddy around," and to "plateau" in their growth and service. Someone needs occasionally to inspire God's people to fresh adventure and sacrifice, to renew their courage to thrust forward, and to remind them again of their high calling. You can do your share of this. You can require expertness, high quality work, and patient endurance of yourself, and thus be an example to co-workers when times of discouragement come. You can instill some "sanctified pride" in work faithfully attempted, in service well done, and in rewards reaped. You can remember to commend persons for their honest effort and to affirm volunteers for work well done.

Periodically Summarize and Predict

Periodically offer some crisp summaries of past achievements, present efforts, and future goals. Persons need this sense of perspective. They can claim progress better if someone summarizes the areas covered, evaluates the efforts of the past, sets the present in a larger context, and points out the direction in which things are moving. God's Spirit hopefully will raise up many prophetic persons who can stand up from time to time to offer summaries. You need not do it all, but you should be ready to do your share of it.

Offer some "cautious forecasts." Often God's prophet has been able to speak to God's people about portents he discerned in the future. All predicting should be done humbly and with full awareness of your own fallibility and finitude. But it is good at times to predict where present trends might possibly lead, to "complete the curve," and to meditate upon the shape of things to come. If you model this for your people, and encourage them in it, they may grow in their ability to test every act and decision in light of its long-range and immediate results.

Harmonize Relationships and Evaluations

Ascertain whether facilities are up to standards. Morale of those in a group can sag if they are trying to sew for the naked with worn-out machines, or are trying to type releases with worn-out typewriters, or are preparing "meals on wheels" to send to the poor with only smoky ovens and stoves to cook on. You will be wise leaders if you balance the needs of society and of people "out there" with the needs of your own people. Watch out for jobs that damage their doers.

Analyze in ways that computers cannot do. Observe the depth of conviction which lies beneath a given objection or plea. Observe the feelings of the person whose "pet opinion" could not be honored. Observe whether remarks began to be directed against persons or against issues. Observe if superlatives were overused, remarks emotion loaded, body language betrayed a mounting tension and anxiety, and whether certain persons lapsed into hurt silence. Observe also if head nodding revealed that a "Spirit-driven-consensus" was about to come, smiles showed a deep satisfaction with what was going on, or a spontaneous sense of joy and celebration came over the meeting. All these and more are the realities you observe carefully.

Listen, Think, and Plan Profoundly

Think more deeply than the novice can, think faster than just everybody can, and think with a deep knowledge of the group's inner life. Begin to develop alternative plans just in case the present plan does not work. Your group need not flounder if you are prepared to "dangle another option" before them when they come to a "dead end."

Focus upon opportunities just a little more than on problems, if you welcome new challenges. Have a childlike trust that God's providential love will lead His people in the future even as

He has done in the past. Your own mood will go a long way to either inspire or to discourage the group.

Train yourself to listen deeply. Try to hear what the person is trying to say but cannot fully express. Read between the lines. Read tones. Read body language. Try to listen as you hope God listens to your prayers—"to the groanings which cannot be uttered." To do this you will need to jerk your mind back from its detours and private agenda, since you can listen 4 or 5 times faster than the person can talk. If your mind did drift off, and you didn't really match meanings with the speaker's mind, you can ask forgiveness for your careless attention, and ask the person to tell you again. Probably the most loving gift you can give to many persons is just your intensive, total, caring, accepting listening.

Be a Good Steward of Your Time

Be keenly aware where your own time goes. Move ahead of (and not behind) deadlines. Study recurring crises and try to ascertain what depth level (and often unexplored) problem seems to lie beneath them all. Often stop and try to approach your task "brand new," just as if you had never met it before.

Lead Out in Times of Repenting and Turning to God

God's Word praised Uzziah's leadership because he treated all God's people like a family. He led the whole nation back to the "family" ordinance of the Passover (2 Kings 23:21-23). He turned to the Lord. He tried to get God's people to return to love their God with their whole heart, soul, mind, and strength. King Hezekiah's leadership, described in 2 Kings 18—20, was praised because he trusted in God, he clung to Jehovah, he recommitted his own life to God as a model for his people. These are biblical models of leadership.

Suggested Readings

Helpful parallel readings may include Peter Drucker's *The Effective Executive,* Harper & Row, 1967, and Lyle E. Schaller and Charles A. Tidwell's *Creative Church Administration,* Abingdon Press, 1975.

Discussion Suggestions

Take a leader's evaluation form or tool which all on the leadership team feel is fair, and then evaluate one another's leadership with it. Have someone experienced in guiding such feedback sessions lead the session in which the team gives each other honest evaluation. Go on to evaluate together how the team is functioning. Keep the tone positive, focused toward growth, building upon one another's gifts and strengths.

21

Plan Many Intergenerational Gatherings

You will be wise to plan many family-of-God gatherings. Try to keep children and adults worshiping together in continuity with the worship patterns of Israel and the early church.

Innocent children cannot really be "the church at worship" when segregated off by themselves. Neither are they "lost" persons who must be made to feel guilty so they can "get saved" during worship, as child evangelism theology asserts. They are "safe" until they reach adult accountability. They can come to God in an acceptable worship. They learn the supremely important realities refreshed in adult worship by sharing with, listening to, and modeling after adults. This is the way they learn all the other life-and-death realities of existence.

You should be prepared for the fears of some that adult worship will be boring. Adult worship will not be boring or incomprehensible to children if adults are really renewing their covenant with their God, and giving account to God here and now for life's pounds and talents, in a service which is a preview of the final judgment day.

If adults move with intense joy, reverence, and awe through celebration of God's greatness and grace, through a fresh examination of what God requires of His pilgrim people, climaxing in a fresh commitment and recommissioning of one another to ministry in the world, then your children will catch the depth and sincerity which is there.

Rather than sending your children off to separate service, where they are taught by flannelgraph, busywork, and a childish theology, parents should begin engaging in the kinds of intense encounters, dramatic activities, and crucial decision-making which belonged to the church worship revealed in the Book of Acts and in the Pastoral Epistles. In the "adults-with-their children" worship services in Acts they made adult decisions while their children listened in, as they would do in family-of-God, house church situations (see chapter 6 on nuclear families).

Believers gathered "to report in", like a football team going into huddle to share signals and get directions for the next play. Sometimes they need to meet the Master, and cry out, "Lord, why could not we cast him out?" Sometimes they wanted to rehearse all that God had done through them.

In the Pastoral Epistles, Timothy's own movement from innocence through nurture in the home, conversion, and sharing in congregational worship is held up as an ideal. And yet the reader never knows whether it was the power of congregational discussions, or testimonies, or preaching services, or prayers, or screening of volunteers, or freeing from taboos, or scrutiny of leaders, or ministering to suffering, or dealing with love of money, or confronting persecution, or exposing the counterfeit— any or all of these might have been little "conversions" along the way during the youthful experiences of Timothy and other young persons like him.

The same series of preaching-teaching-discussion-decision meetings serve to acquaint converts (or your children) with sacred writings, to call them to a salvation commitment, and at the same time to equip adult members for every good work of witness in the world, (2 Timothy 3:15-16). Evangelizing the unbeliever and children, and equipping the church member for mission seem to be blended into one.

When your gatherings for preaching-teaching-discussion-decision actually engage in reproof and correction (2 Timothy 3:16); discern the qualifications of a member to serve as deacon or bishop (1 Timothy 3:1-13); decide which widow should receive mutual aid (1 Timothy 5:1-16); how to intercede for a given king in a certain situation (1 Timothy 2:2); decide which "silly myths" of their culture they must refuse (1 Timothy 1:4 and 4:6-7); hear the prophets give their utterances or see hands of commissioning laid upon a certain member (1 Timothy 4:14); see two or three witnesses bring a charge against one of the congregational elders and watch as the leader is treated fairly and tenderly through it all (1 Timothy 5:19); witness the solemn ceremonies of the laying-on-of-hands in binding-and-loosing baptism or commissioning services, (1 Timothy 5:22); watch as slave and master interact as equals in the congregation, rebuke the businessman who tries to make godliness a means of gain (1 Timothy 6:5) ... when gatherings have such content and reality, then participants are drawn in deeply.

Likely some of your children observers will long to be a fellowship of such beauty and mutual helpfulness. It is possible also that some mere shallow triflers will be frightened away! In God's family, faith is not so much belief in a doctrine of justification, but it is faithfulness in being a new community of God's love and grace. While sharing in a New Testament type service of worship your children are really learning. If they can be seated with their parents in closeness, loving warmth, and a sense of belonging, the worship service may become for them a time when good and great things happen.

Take Seriously the Example-Setting You Can Do

Believe that your own personal examples will have great power. One of Paul's highest hopes was that "in me first, for a pattern, God might display His perfect Fatherly patience" (1 Timothy 1:16). One way or another you are modeling something about what it means to be a member of God's family. If God's family is first in your priorities, your brothers and sisters will feel this quiet influence. If you speak diligently of God's will for His children when you lie down, when you rise up, when you walk by the way, and can do so with an easy naturalness, the living example will be a powerful influence.

Do not hesitate to share your successes and failures with the congregation you help to lead. Let them know you are human. Admit frankly where you see yourself coming short. People will accept your leadership better if you do not try to deny your humanness, nor try to cover up the fact that you fail and come short. It will be important if, after you have frankly admitted that "I have not attained and I am not perfect" you also go on and assert truthfully, "but I follow after passionately, that I may lay hold upon that for which I have been laid hold of by Jesus Christ" (Philippians 3:12).

You will be wise to reserve the most intimate facts about your failures for a small group of trusted peers, who have entered a covenant of absolute confidentiality. In such a group you can risk transparency and honesty in "confessing your faults one to another and praying one for another." There you can "walk out into the light as He is in the light so that the blood of Jesus Christ, God's Son, can go on cleansing from sin." If, however, you share too many intimate details of your personal or inner life's shortcomings before a congregation containing immature children, new converts, and seekers, you may overload their fantasies and slow down their growth at their own frontiers.

Expect Spiritual Renewal Through Administrative Efforts
You will be wise to develop an attitude of quiet expectancy toward ways God can use your administration to bring renewal and release His blessings. Entirely too many people feel that only their charismatic gift of healing or miracles, or of tongues or of prophesy (or one of the more spectacular gifts) can be used of God to bring renewal and blessing. In contrast to this you can learn to expect God to work through your gifts of administration. God wants to bless your "ad-ministering" as well as your ministering, that is, your facilitating the ministries of others as well as your direct ministry to persons. God can honor your

enabling of others, serving humbly behind the scenes, as well as when you serve in the limelight.

Try to regard your administration as making vital participation possible. Look upon your necessary committee meetings as times you are trying to upgrade the cooperation of many Christians. You are trying constantly to help God's family to behave like a family. You are concerned that they enjoy to behave like a family. You are concerned that they learn God's standards for His family. You want them to know and to enter into their royal privileges as heirs of their Father-King of the universe. You hope they will break bread together as God's family, regard their congregation as their spiritual kin, sacrifice for one another like a family, be partial to one another as a family. Your watchword as you administer might well be "do good to all men, and especially to those who are of the household of faith." By your administration you help brothers and sisters to find what they are to do for each other especially. What is special about their interaction with congregational members, beyond that which they do for the members of any other group they belong to?

As a servant-brother-or-sister-in-God's-family, you will need to resist constantly the worldly models in which leaders lord it over one another, and leaders higher in the line-and-staff hierarchy can be benefactors to persons beneath them.

You will likely feel the constant seduction of the corporation models or the country club models of administration so much admired by the person on the street. You will be wise to regard them as demonic temptations, as Isaiah's servant did when he turned away from the mere nationalistic model (Isaiah 41:8) and the kingship model (Isaiah 41:25), choosing instead the servant model (Isaiah 42). Your model can be Christ who refused the hierarchy models and materialistic-success models (Matthew 4:1-11).

Be Satisfied Even with Small Changes

Often you will need to be satisfied with just a few changes, a series of small steps, rather than the massive changes and the glorious renewal you can dream about. If you try to change too many things too soon, you may create division in the congregation. A few good changes come by rapid revolution, but more often the most healing, durable, and peaceful changes come by evolution.

If by a review of your five-year trends, and a fresh study of the Scriptures or your historic confessions of faith, you become convinced that there is a certain direction of change which God desires for His people, you can suggest a series of sermons, studies, or discussions which accentuate the discontent with the status quo. After convictions are awakened, seek for consensus among the concerned as to some next steps.

As leaders you will be wise to plan for information sharing. You may try to get your agreed-upon goal for change down to one or two specific goals which are almost quantifiable, so people can see whether they are reaching their goal. You may be wise to have an initiating group or task force carrying central responsibility all the way through.

You will be well advised to check with conference leaders as you go along, and to seek counsel from leaders of other congregations who have tried to reach a goal and achieve a change somewhat similar to yours. Be sure to keep the budget out in the open, with methods of fund-raising completely approved. Often in the budget raising is where secret resistances are helped to come out into the open.

In seeking to be change agents, be realistic about time schedules, and establish cut-off points along the way. Then stop and reconsider your progress thus far. Share any small successes. Be open to "serendipity" or leadings which come as surprises to all of you. Build in self-correction by clear feedback. Let any critics or persons who are dragging their feet know that you hear and respect their feelings. Take more time for the process if disunity threatens.

Be sure to claim and consolidate real gains. Regard any changes as merely obedience for now, and as merely another step along the unending way of discipleship.

Regard Your Congregation as a "Living System"

You will be wise to regard the subgroups of your congregations as parts of the "living systems" of the congregation. You can expect that when God's Spirit moves in power through the nurture commission (or other subsystem) of the congregation, all the other systems will be effected. If, however, the nurture commission is cold, lazy, or divided, the entire congregation will suffer.

As a leadership team you have the high calling of shepherding, coordinating, and balancing out the work of many subsystems (committees and commissions) of the entire larger congregational system. You will likely watch with prayers and fascination as one commission of the congregation gets "turned on" about their task. First they may go through a brainstorming stage. After that they may move through a stage when shared goals begin to merge. A stage may come when standards and determinations and convictions take shape. Hopefully they will move on into the stage when real actions follow.

Don't be surprised if a vitally functioning subsystem of your congregation creates some new symbols of their shared life and convictions. Be glad when you see the personal needs of individuals being met as they pour out their lives for group goals. For instance, a formerly cold Christian may find a vital prayer life while caught up in the activities of the fellowship commission.

Your function, as a leadership team, can be that of catalyst. You can perform a connecting function. You can mediate. You can endorse and back up the subgroup which is moving courageously. You can share some of your own vision. You can help link the work of one commission or subsystem to the larger congregation.

Let High Expectations Inspire and Renew You

Church members want you to be faithful to your tasks: to finish what you start, to relate warmly to persons with opposing views, not to cringe before "success-symbol" people, and not to allow your own emotional bias to cloud your judgment. Can you live in reciprocal subordination to your peers?

Church members hope you will show flexibility of spirit, that you will bounce back from discouraging experiences, that you adjust well to new people and situations, and that you serve with a good mixture of seriousness and joy. They hope you will evidence Holy Spirit life and power. Are you known for this fruit of the Spirit?

Church members hope you will keep your integrity under pressure, that you will refuse to compromise your convictions, that you will be a person of your word, and that you will relate fairly to those who precede or follow you in a given task. Are you known as persons faithful in responsibilities assigned to you?

Christians you serve hope you will be humble enough to admit your own limitations, that you will be able to admit it when you really do not know, that you will apologize when you have goofed or hurt someone, and that you will still believe that the forces of good are greater than the forces of evil. Can you admit your errors and failures forthrightly?

Christians you serve will want you to have your human family back of you in your work and will hope you are a good Christian at home. They will expect you to have an exemplary family life and to keep commitments made to your spouse and children, if you have such. How do the people in your human family feel about your performance in God's family—the congregation?

Church members for whom you administer will hope that you will be a good listener, that you will be able to show empathy and caring for persons under stress, and that you will work to rally support for grieving persons or those handicapped. Do they see you as a tactful insightful counselor?

Church members hope you will have the skill of building a warmly caring community, that you will nurture good traditions, that you will foster mutual trust and respect, and that you will try to win back those alienated or offended. They hope you are a person of prayer and that you mediate God's forgiving love through your relationships. Do you have a proven ability to reconcile enemies into friends?

Members for whom you administer will expect you to show tact and skill in coping with conflict, in securing two-sided scrutiny of an issue, in being fair to the minority, and in relating the conflict to deep principles of Christian faith. They hope you can facilitate good problem-solving sequences. Can you help your group to detect what is seeming good to the Holy Spirit and to the group?

Church members hope you will be a clear thinker, who can state profound truths simply, who knows relevant facts to bring to bear upon problems, and who believes the gospel is relevant to all of life. They hope you sense your place in the kingdom of God. Can you accept Christ's lifestyle as a pattern for your personal life and His teachings as normative for persons in your congregation?

Church members hope that you believe deeply in true worship and in genuinely Christian fellowship, that you will be able to relate well to children and to youth, and that you can help promote programs which capture their interest and deepen their commitment to Christ. Can you avoid "gnat-straining," keep a sense of humor, and keep entering God's kingdom in a childlike spirit?

Church members hope that you can relate warmly to denominational leaders and that you can relate ecumenically to other Christians in the area and tactfully to community leaders. Can you care about worldwide missions even as you serve in your part of Christ's mission?

Church members hope that you possess evangelistic warmth, that you welcome persons to church and to Christ, and that you can help to administer a program of congregational life which draws persons to Christ by both word and deed.

Suggested Readings

Parallel readings may include books like the one by Alvin J. Lindgren and Norman L. Shawchuck, *Management for Your Church,* Abingdon Press, 1977, or one by E. Mansell Pattison, *Pastor and Parish: A Systems Approach,* Fortress Press, 1977.

Discussion Suggestions

As a leadership team, discuss together the suggestions of chapter 21. First claim as strengths all the areas in which it is clear you are doing well. Then list areas for improvement and adopt a plan for improvement. Keep working together until practical next steps are agreed upon. Keep expecting spiritual renewal to be sparked in your congregation through renewal in your own life together as a leadership team.

22

Expect God's Leading

Expect God to Lead You Issue by Issue

Often you may long for the security of a book of rules, a set of laws, a creed, or a master plan. It will be hard for you to find the way into the future step by step. But at each new step of faith, each new consensus as to what the way of faithfulness and obedience is for you and for your people you will be implicitly renewing your covenant to go on being God's family. This is partly what it means to be a non-creedal church, but to be one which repeatedly "confesses its faith."

Your nearest thing to a rulebook is God's family album, the Scriptures. As leaders you will be wise to back up and review (in the Scriptures) God's ways of calling, guiding, purifying, and using His people, His family, in days that are past. As you and your people pause and do corporate exposition of the Scriptures, seeking for light on your current problems, you will find the way.

As you seek to be God's family now, reflect carefully about the ways God led His people into covenant with Himself and with one another. Notice how He rescued them during crises, called them to a life of purity and holiness, cautioned them against merely copying their surrounding culture, helped them to test false spirits, to hear their true prophets, to forgive one another after failure, and to help failing members to begin again. He helped them to interpret their Scriptures, to select their gifted members for ministry, and to send members upon missions of outreach. He helped them to claim their family reality before Him as heavenly Father and to hope for their eternal and heavenly home. The new people, the family of God that He was able to create and call together became itself part of God's good news for His world.

A running start in holy history will likely be your first approach to every issue. As you move along you yourselves will be developing a tradition, a pattern, of "how we do things as God's family." This tradition could become a binding legalism if it prevents God's newness, and His fresh adventure, but tradition can also be a source of stability.

Do Not Merely Rely on Compromise or the Golden Mean

Because I have quite often suggested that you will find widely polarized opinions among your members, and that you will be wise to seek for some high road between the extremes, I do not want to suggest that Aristotle's golden mean, or a mere middle of the road, is always the way. Often you will need to take firm positions as a leadership team, and take your turns being prophetic. Also God may need to lead both you as a team and all of your people to a new repentance and a way through which none of you had envisioned.

I cherish the conviction that a consensus led by God's Spirit can be a highest common denominator, rather lowest common denominator as compromises tend to be. I cherish the hope, based upon the Scriptures and recent church experiences, that leaders can find "win-win" solutions when a synthesis is found which incorporates the best in two previously held polarities. Something which "seems good to the Holy Ghost and to us" can be obviously wiser and better for everybody than anything anyone had glimpsed when they came to the meeting. Admittedly such sacred experiences of "Spirit-led-consensus" are all too rare, but they should remain a goal of every church leader.

Blending Family Loyalties Will Require Tact and Skill

Although Christ sometimes warned that unless His followers placed loyalty to His new family above their loyalties to their human and biological families, they could not be His disciples, yet He also warned His followers not to say "it is Corban," or dedicated to God's cause, and so be relieved from their duty to support their biological parents. Christ insisted that both loyalties be taken very seriously. He did not hesitate to put "the Father's business" above family pressures when He was twelve years old, and He placed His Father's call above His mother's advice during His early miracles and ministry. But even in His dying hours He showed again that no kingdom business could make Him forget His duties to His mother. We are called to follow in His steps in His way of combining and blending family loyalties.

The Apostle Paul echoed Christ's insistence that a person "has denied the faith and is worse than an infidel" if duties and loyalties to biological family are ignored. Yet Paul by his own example repeatedly placed church work ahead of home and family. As leaders you will find yourselves constantly trying to decrease the competition between strong family life and strong congregational life and trying to increase the cooperation between these two centers of life and loyalty.

You will never escape this tension entirely. If you expand the duties of leadership team, elders, deacons, or church council members to the point where they spend many hours together wrestling with the issues of the present and the light the Scriptures shed upon these issues, then their human family life might suffer. Beware that you don't rear a generation of children who halfway hate the church because it was the successful rival for dad/or mother's prime time!

You may be wise, in your own families and as a recommendation for all the human families within your larger household of God, to practice an alternation in prioritizing your time. Possibly some nights of the week should be free from church duties and committees so that families can share prime

time around their own firesides. Then other evenings could be
family-of-God nights when the entire human family goes
together to family night at the church. If there could be something intergenerational, and also something for every age-group,
this might help the whole human family to want to go. It will be
important that children grow up loving both their families, their
human one and their divine one, their biological one and the one
God offers through His saving Son.

If and as you are skillful in blending and balancing the
loyalties and contributions of church family and human family,
of the family of God and the biological family, you will be
greatly enriching both. The human, biological families of your
congregation will be immensely enriched by having a congregational extended family near by, and by having the church as
God's realm of redemption encircling their biological family
(which is God's realm of creation). Likewise the family of God
(the congregation) will be enriched by having strong biological
families within it.

If you can't always separate the two, and be sure when
God's Spirit is leading and working through the biological
families of your congregation and when He is leading through
the whole family of God, don't worry about this. Paul couldn't
quite figure it all out either. In Ephesians 5:15-33 when he discussed how suffering love for one another (love like Christ has
for the church) should pervade relationships, he says in glad
amazement "this is a great mystery."

Discussion Suggestions

As leaders you doubtless know well the human families that
make up your "household-of-God" congregation. Discuss how
your families serve the congregation's life, and how your congregation serves your families. Look for evidences of competition
for the prime time of parents. Notice especially the families led
by single parents, or the singles and widows living alone. Is there
a way to have the "covenant-love" of God's caring household
flow around and enrich the lives of any who may be lonely?

Appendix A
Brief Form for Writing a Proposal (See Chapter 4)

I. What is a proposal?

A. A proposal is a brief (one page if possible) recommendation to improve, create, solve, resolve, etc., a situation.

B. A proposal should be offered to one's boss, peers, or subordinates in time for the above purpose with the clear understanding that it can be discussed, altered, rejected, accepted, chewed, digested, or rewritten in part or in whole many times.

C. A proposal takes a gripe, complaint, or criticism and suggests solutions rather than enjoying to see trouble and criticism extended.

D. A proposal is a way to move an idea along an action track toward achievement. Too often good ideas are lost, stolen, or disfigured because they are not nurtured (proposed to the right people).

E. A proposal assists individuals and groups to:

(1) Move from a brainstorming session to action.
(2) Move from a circular dead center paralysis to purposeful direction.
(3) Identify leadership from dependency.
(4) Save time and clearly identify what aspect(s) of a good

idea needs further work rather than making one or more people feel their good ideas are not appreciated.
(5) Grasp another person's ideas easily.
(6) Discuss an action plan with less anxiety.
(7) Reduce confusion and hostility.

II. Planning outline for a proposal (all of these items may not be necessarily included in all proposals but they should be evaluated as to their importance before being left off).

To:	(One's boss, team, subordinates, any other)
From:	(Person, persons writing proposal)
Date:	(Date proposal is written)
Re:	(Indicate subject of proposal)
Why?	Problem to be solved, ideas created, etc., by proposal.
What?	Specific change, task, expectation, request, assignment, event or activity, specific objectives, and goals.
Who?	1. Who will do the work? Specific tasks? 2. Who will be affected directly, indirectly? 3. Who will be invited, not invited, or included? 4. How many? 5. Who will be involved?
When?	1. Date of the "what" above will go into effect or be produced 2. When response, revision, answer is needed
How?	Methods and procedures, program design, promotion, the steps involved, how will it really work?
How much?	Budget—including time, material costs, and how funds can be raised or found to pay for expenditures.
Where?	1. Place(s) 2. Specific room arrangements 3. Directions for getting there 4. Procedure for getting "in"
How well?	1. Evaluation methods 2. Revisions 3. Future projections

Appendix B

The Congregation as the Family of God (Chapters 6 ff.)

A Possible Family of God Model of Congregational Life

Introduction

In each house church one or two members are selected by gift discernment to represent the group in each area of concern, 1 through 6.

1. Justice and Peace on Earth

The heavenly Father eternally intended that His children should live together in love. In spite of many prodigals, He kept calling together a priestly people, His family. God's family is to model for all humanity what Father's will and plan is. God's people are to decide what is right and wrong in their own times, and declare this.

This commission would deal with such issues as war, peace, the draft, war taxes, ecology, development, poverty, abortion, race, injustices, etc.

2. Missions and Evangelism

The Father ever invites prodigals back to His family, through the new birth. His creating of His new people, His family, is itself part of the good news. Unless His people live the news, their gospel is not really true. Conversion begins when prodigals decide to join this social wholeness, His family.

This commission would provide leadership in such areas as information on world missions, methods of local outreach, and training in friendship evangelism.

3. Mutual Aid

Father's children relay Father's forgiveness and love to one another, and are vulnerable. In their life together they show the difference when Jesus (not Mammon or Mars) is Lord. Children in God's family rejoice with those who do rejoice, and weep with those who weep. Children peer-counsel one another about issues faced in service in the world.

This commission could plan programs for elderly, disabled, retarded, etc. Crisis ministries to one another. Peer counseling training and service.

4. Nurture

Little children learn family of God ethics by watching adults decide ethical issues. Intergenerational dramas from biblical history help children live into peoplehood. The exposited word of Scripture is constantly injected into the search for consensus. Human families decide ethical issues, at home, much as the congregation does it.

This commission would coordinate the nurture and education program through such activities as intergenerational discussions, dramas, training in storytelling, Sunday school, and teacher training.

5. Worship

Through storytelling, biblical dramas, exposition, the Father's grace is told and retold. The broad way and the narrow way are described, and worshipers renew covenants. Reconsecrations may focus on faithfulness in current ethical issues and on stewardship. God's children recommission one another to service out in God's world.

This commission would plan the spiritual diet for the year. Celebrations of the church year. House churches lead group at times.

6. Elders

Elders confer and coordinate the congregation's consideration and decision-making of the issues of unity, worship, nurture, social justice, and faithfulness. They carry their consensus to house church and small groups for processing and in turn carry the small group's consensus, or questions, to their elder's meetings. Periodically the entire congregation gathers for binding-and-loosing decisions.

The elders hear reports from house churches, coordinate congregational deciding, carry through goal setting, and self-study.

7. Preacher-Teacher-Equipper

Because the Scriptures (Family Album) are central, servants of the

Word serve centrally. The congregation sets apart and charges one (or several) to "give themselves to the Word." Depth level study of the Scriptures precedes the exposition-preaching of worship. "Position papers" on ethical issues may equip God's ministering people for their service.

The preacher-teacher-equipper team exposits the Scriptures in worship, does teacher-training in use of Scripture, and prepares position papers on current issues.

Appendix C
Support in a Face-to-Face Group (Chapter 6)

Definition of Support
  "*Sub-portare*" means "to get under so as to help carry; to keep from falling or sinking; to give strength to...."

Assumption
  Support in a group must alternate between the help the individual gives to the group and the help the group gives to the individual.

A. How the Individual May Support the Group
   1. Affirm its declared purpose and objective by joining it, rising with trust and openness.

   2. Assist the group in updating its declared objective, respecting its history and tradition.

   3. Determine the emergent objectives of other members and respect them, regarding some diversity as an enrichment.

   4. Blend individual objectives into a composite goal for the group, seeking the highest common denominator.

   5. Blend individual loyalty intentions into a group covenant, making the highest intentions become more explicit.

   6. Defend the group against its critics and competing loyalties.

B. How the Group May Support the Individual

1. Provide mutual aid in times of distress.
2. Assist the individual to reach his or her personal goals by affirming the person's identity and uniqueness.
3. Provide balance for the individual's one-sidedness by the loving use of "critical leveling."
4. Assist in the solving of personal problems as a fellowship of binding-and-loosing discernment.
5. Provide fellowship in relaxation, recreation, and fun in ways which are aesthetic, ethical, and enriching.
6. Assist both inward growth and outward vision and service by celebrating newly made commitments.
7. Discern and help to develop a spiritual gift for ministry, and remove blocks to communication and service.
8. Help to test vocational calls or redirections and change by holding group counseling sessions upon request.
9. Commission to service, and prayer support in it.

Appendix D
Shepherding the Congregation as a Living System (Chapter 8)

System is defined as something vitally interdependent, much as the circulatory system of the human body.

I. *What Membership in the System Requires*
   1. Many face-to-face interactions
   2. Strong emotional intensities
   3. Positive feelings about membership
   4. The receiving of genuine benefits
   5. Reciprocal giving and receiving

II. *Marks of a Living Church System*
   1. It is creating symbols
   2. It has "holism" (more than sum of its parts)
   3. It functions in an open "synergy" (group goals meet individual ones too)
   4. It is an "isomorphism" (a unique "body" is being created)
   5. It functions as God's "extended family" system
   6. It asserts priority over other systems (business, school, government)

III. *How Subsystems Support One Another*
   1. The proclaiming system
   2. The symbolizing subsystem
   3. The moralizing subsystem (generally accepted standards and taboos)

4. The learning-growth subsystem
5. The reparative subsystem (healing and restoring)
6. By affirming the "thou shalts" of the Beatitudes
7. By affirming the "thou shalt nots" of the Ten Commandments

IV. *Possible Developmental Stages of a Church System*

1. The "storming" stage (people act ad-hoc, are uncommitted)
2. The "forming" stage (shared goals and ties emerge)
3. The "norming" stage (standards take shape)
4. The "performing" stage (people work together for common goals)
5. The church provides fellowship, and connections with the "outside world"

V. *Functions of the Preacher-Teacher-Equipper*

1. Points to Christ, the Head of the system
2. The intentionality function (helping persons to consciously choose)
3. The catalyst-connecting function
4. The facilitating-mediating function
5. The modeling and risk-taking function
6. Sharing responsibility, authority, and control
7. Symbolizing the system's memory and identity (calling to self-awareness)

Suggested Readings

E. Mansell Pattison, *Pastor and Parish, A Systems Approach,* Fortress, Press, 1977, and A. Lindgren and N. Shawchock, *Management For Your Church,* Abingdon Press, 1977.

Appendix E

Methods Which May Grieve the Holy Spirit and Prevent a Spirit-Driven Consensus (Chapter 9)

It is unethical—

1. To close the "agenda for the day" without allowing the opposing viewpoint to be heard.
2. To withhold crucial sources of information when it's against one's bias.
3. To use humor to "laugh off" an issue which deserves serious decision.
4. To place unfavored issues at the close of the agenda, so "the logic of fatigue" operates when they come up.
5. To allow the group to work on "hidden agenda" only and never alert them to that fact.
6. To delegate authority only to those on one's own side; to exaggerate differences.
7. To summarize "selected facts" which retread one's own bias; call for a vote after only one side is presented.
8. To allow comments of opposing view to go "unlinked," unsummarized.
9. To rephrase own side so as to accent, and opposing side so as to soften or belittle..
10. To make own desired goal an ethical issue, and an opposing one an "adiaphoron" (it doesn't really matter).
11. To appeal to one's own "vast experience" and so intimidate the novice.
12. To make it appear that "cards are stacked" in favor of one's chosen solution.

13. To retreat into parliamentary law, technicalities, when one wants to halt action.
14. To "turn on the charm" so as to get one's own way; caricature the opposition.
15. To select for emphasis only those facts which support one's own side of a discussion.
16. To seat persons in "less favorable seats" who oppose one's own preference.
17. To use "techniques of argument" only on one's own side of the case; overuse emotion-loaded words.
18. To trace "handwriting on the wall" in favor of own preferences, and against one's opponents.
19. To drop in component parts of an idea, by suggestion, so it emerges later on as "their idea."
20. To "drop important names," use testimonials, and hint that "sources close to the administration say. . . ."
21. To use "loud protest on minor points" so as to hide disunity on deep issues.
22. To sacrifice someone's rights so as to gain efficiency; achieve the program.
23. To tell some "polite lies" so as to help someone "save face."
24. To use a little flattery so members feel good, and assume they are being creative.
25. To copy the method which politicians call "lobbying" or "log rolling."
26. To "suffer it to be so now," to be authoritarian because people want it and seem to need it.
27. To delay an opposing move by veiled warnings of "this dangerous precedent."
28. To pretend to speak for an "invisible committee"—"they say."

Appendix F
Group Decision-Making (Chapter 9)

1. Does there seem to be an expectation of a "group concensus," a wisdom of the group to emerge?
2. Are any periods of silence regarded as awkward failures; or as creative periods of incubation?
3. Do issues which deserve a two-sided treatment get it?
4. Trace any differences which emerge to notice how they are finally dealt with.
5. Is the group moving through a problem-solving process methodically?
6. Is anyone being scapegoated?
7. Are the rational comments and dialogue "saying" the same thing the relationships are "saying?"
8. Are persons responding to the "feeling tone" of one another's remarks, or to words only?
9. Are there times when "the lure of formal procedures" hinders the real progress?
10. Is the "mirror reaction" working; are people being influenced by nonverbal cues?
11. Are any "star formations" forming (satellites orbiting around a strong leader)?
12. Are any persons "playing roles"; striking a pose?
13. If there is an "unnoticed election" going on, who is the group choosing as their leader?
14. Is the group attributing power to anyone; doing obeisance to anyone? Is this member using it?

15. Does the group ever seek to achieve an inner esprit de corps by attacking an outgroup?
16. Do remarks seem to be "person centered," rather than "issue centered?"
17. Are there any evidences of any hostilities being projected upon a "father figure"?
18. Is the group being hindered by the lack of a recognized or appointed leader?
19. In what ways might the presence of a good leader have improved the group process?
20. Do the group members seem to be aware that they are being watched?

Appendix G
Group Building and Task Functions (Chapters 9-11)

I observed your participation in the _____ group

on_____, 19__.
   (month)

I saw you performing these GROUP BUILDING FUNCTIONS

Encouraging—

Being friendly, warm, responsive to others, praising others and their ideas, agreeing with and accepting the contributions of others.

Mediating—

Harmonizing, conciliating differences in points of view, making compromises.

Gatekeeping—

Trying to make it possible for another member to make a contribution by saying, "We haven't heard from Jim yet," or suggesting limited talking-time for everyone so that all will have a chance to be heard.

Standard setting—

Expressing standards for the group to use in choosing its subject matter or procedures, rules of conduct, ethical values.

Following—

Going along with the group, somewhat passively accepting the ideas of others, serving as an audience during group discussion, being a good listener.

Relieving tension— Draining off negative feeling by humor, throwing oil on troubled waters, diverting attention from unpleasant to pleasant matters, calling attention to positive and hopeful aspects.

I saw you performing these GROUP TASK FUNCTIONS

Initiating— Suggesting new ideas or a changed way of looking at the group problem or goal, proposing new activities.

Information seeking— asking for relevant facts or authoritative information.

Information giving— Providing relevant facts or authoritative information or relating personal experience pertinent to the group task.

Opinion giving— Stating a pertinent belief or opinion about something the group is considering.

Clarifying— Probing for meaning and understanding, restating something the group is considering.

Elaborating— Building on a previous comment, enlarging on it, giving examples.

Coordinating— Showing or clarifying the relationships among various ideas, trying to pull ideas and suggestions together, linking them.

Orienting— Defining the progress of the discussion in terms of the group's goals, raising questions about the direction the discussion is taking.

Testing— Checking with the group to see if it is ready to make a decision or to take some action.

Summarizing— Reviewing the content of past discussion, claiming gains already made.

Observation Instrument

The purpose of this exercise is to sharpen your observation of the various behaviors that help groups work. Sometimes these are called leadership functions, but you will see that they can be provided by any member.

Rolls   **Names**

I. Group-Building Functions

    Encouraging

    Harmonizing

    Gatekeeping

    Trusting and Leveling

    Compromising

II. Group Task Functions

    Initiating

    Seeking Information

    Informing or Giving Opinions

    Clarifying

    Consensus Testing

    Summarizing

Rating a Leader's Behavior (Chapters 9-11)

Very poor	1	2	3	4	5	Very good
1. Little awareness of history of the group						Fully informed on group's history
2. Little awareness of belief strength in group						Aware of belief strength on the issue
3. Little loyalty to cause of the group						Full loyalty to group's cause
4. Unenthusiastic, apathetic						Contagious enthusiasm
5. Cool and aloof attitude						Friendliness and affection
6. Insensitive to feelings of the group						Keenly sensitive to feelings
7. Committed to the status quo						Ready for adventure
8. Quick to resent any show of hostility						Able to absorb hostility
9. Unable to verbalize the goals of the group						Able to verbalize the group's goals
10. Unimaginative as to new solutions						Highly imaginative
11. Unable to offer structures for group decision						Able to facilitate group decision
12. Unable to use humor tactfully						Skilled use of humor
13. Unable to detect subverbal cues						Able to sense what is going on
14. Sees only a few of the group members						Uses wide "peripheral vision"
15. Shows partiality						Is fair and impartial
16. Accents the gloomy and negative						Accents the pleasant and positive
17. Allows a "hidden agenda" to operate						Keeps real issues in the open

Leadership Functions and Skills

1. Fails to provide for comfort of the group
2. Fails to define key terms
3. Allows members to remain strangers
4. Allows issue to remain unclear
5. Allows limits of freedom to be undefined
6. Allows one-sided presentation of issues
7. Uses emotion-loaded words
8. Allows "discussion hogs" to dominate
9. Allows some persons to be unenlisted
10. Allows unclarity to persist
11. Allows parallel ideas to go unlinked
12. Offers no help to summarize progress
13. Answers many questions himself
14. Offers no sources of information
15. Allows minority to be abused
16. Performs all leader's functions himself
17. Uses parliamentary law legalistically
18. Uses no tests for emerging agreement

Provides for group's comfort
Defines key terms
Helps members become acquainted
Helps clarify the issue
Defines limits of group's authority
Secures two-sided presentation
Avoids emotion-loaded words
Curbs overtalkative members
Enlists silent member
Helps rephrase to clarify
Links parallel ideas
Helps summarize group progress
Reflects questions back to the group
Suggests sources of information
Protects rights of minority
Shares leadership functions
Seeks group consensus and unity
Checks for amount of agreement

Appendix I
Feedback (Chapters 9-11)

Name	Group	Meeting Number

"Feedback" is a way of helping another person to consider changing his behavior. It is communication to a person (or a group) which gives that person information about how he or she affects, is experienced by others. As in a guided missile system feedback helps an individual keep behavior "on target" and thus better achieve his or her goals. If done amidst Christian caring and concern, it becomes "family admonition."

Below are listed eight criteria of useful feedback. Rate the feedback which usually occurs in your group on each of the eight scales by circling the appropriate number. You may also want to make some notes on each criterion, such as particular instances which you remember from your group.

1. It is *descriptive* rather than evaluative. It does not say behavior was either good or bad. By describing one's own reaction, it leaves the individual free to use it or not to use it as he or she sees fit. By avoiding evaluative language, it reduces the need for the individual to respond defensively.

Descriptive   1   2   3   4   5   6   Evaluative

Instances:

2. It is *specific* rather than general. To be told that one is "dominating" will probably not be as useful as to be told that "just now when we were deciding the issue, you did not listen to what others said, and I felt forced to accept your arguments or face attack from you."

Specific   1   2   3   4   5   6   General

Instances:

3. It *takes into account the needs of both the receiver and giver* of feedback. Feedback can be destructive when it serves only our own needs and fails to consider the needs of the person on the receiving end. Feedback is "mid-course correction" for the receiver.

Takes needs   1   2   3   4   5   6   Does not take
of both into   needs of both
account   into account

Instances:

4. It is *directed toward behavior which the receiver can do something about.* Frustration is only increased when a person is reminded of some shortcoming over which he or she has no control, such as "You remind me of . . ." or "You are too tall."

Directed toward   1   2   3   4   5   6   Directed toward
modifiable   nonmodifiable
behavior   behavior

Instances

5. It is *solicited,* rather than imposed. Feedback is most useful when the receiver has formulated the kind of question which those observing can answer, if he or she admits the problem.

Solicited   1   2   3   4   5   6   Imposed

Instances:

6. It is *well-timed.* In general, feedback is most useful not a long while later, but at the earliest opportunity after the given behavior (depending, of course, on the person's readiness to hear it, support available from others, etc.).

Well-timed   1   2   3   4   5   6   Poorly timed

Instances:

7. It is *checked* to insure clear communication. One way of doing this is to have the receiver try to rephrase the feedback received to see if it corresponds to what the sender had in mind.

Checked   1 2 3 4 5 6   Not checked
with sender   with sender

Instances:

8. When feedback is given in a training group, both giver and receiver have opportunity to *check with others* in the group the accuracy of the feedback. Is this one man's impression or an impression shared by others? "Did you hear him as I did?"

Checked   1 2 3 4 5 6   Not checked
with others   with others

Instances:

Appendix J
Was Our Committee Meeting Today Healthy or Sick?
(Chapters 9-11)

Post-meeting Evaluation Form—Check on Each Continuum Line

Very healthy	An average group	Very sick
1. All the members speak up about what they think	1. A few members do all the talking	
2. Decisions are worked through until a general consensus of agreement is reached	2. Most members mumble assent	
3. Well-informed members contribute ideas in the area of their competence	3. Competent people sit silently by	
4. A member's value is judged by the merit of his idea	4. New people with good ideas are not listened to	

5. The whole group handles questions that concern the whole group	5. Decision-making is quickly referred to committees
6. Major issues get major time	6. Minor issues consume the major time
7. Major issues evoke mature approaches to change and "working through"	7. Minor and simple issues make people seethe and boil
8. Minor issues are settled with the attention they deserve	8. Major issues are passed over
9. Decisions reached by thorough participation are final and satisfactory	9. The same subjects, supposedly settled, keep coming up again
10. Members really understand one another's ideas, plans, and proposals	10. Quick judgments are passed on issues people do not understand
11. Members objectively center interest on goals and tasks	11. Members subjectively talk about people in scapegoating

12. The group carries forward in the performance of tasks and the achievement of goals

12. The group accomplishes little in absence of the chairman

13. The group works goalwise toward change

13. The group is afraid of change

14. Rewards and criticism are shared

14. Rewards and criticism are concentrated in a few

15. Initiative and responsibility are encouraged by growth in a sense of personal confidence, competence, and worth

15. Initiative and responsibility are stifled by dependence

16. Search for help from all sources is continuous

16. No resources outside the group are drawn upon

17. Information is fed back into the group

17. Little is told to the group

18. The worth of persons is respected

18. The person is squelched in expression and stunted in growth

19. Experience is considered the occasion for growth in responsibility and love

19. Action lacks altitude and depth, remaining on the horizontal plane without vertical relationships to God

20. Action is God-related

20. Action is self-centered

—Paul F. Douglas, *The Group Workshop Way in the Church* (Association Press, New York) pp. 13, 14.

Appendix K
My Participation Profile as a Group Member (Chapters 9-11)

Very poorly   **Very Well**

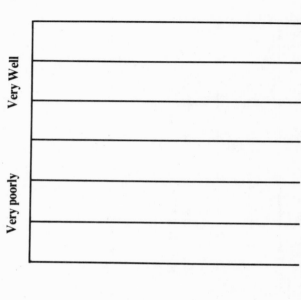

1. I prepared in advance so that I could participate

2. I tried to get to know the group members

3. I maintained a cooperative attitude

4. I acknowledged the ideas of others

5. I stated my ideas clearly

6. I gave reasons for objections I raised

7. I avoided using emotionally loaded words

8. I helped the group get all the facts

9. I took only my share of the time

10. I helped to draw out silent members

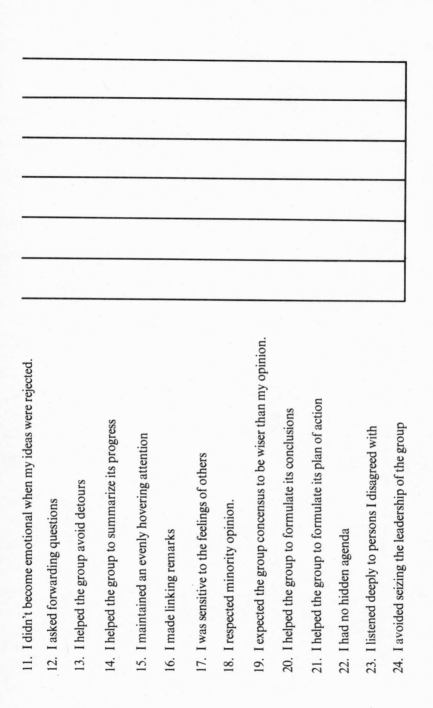

11. I didn't become emotional when my ideas were rejected.

12. I asked forwarding questions

13. I helped the group avoid detours

14. I helped the group to summarize its progress

15. I maintained an evenly hovering attention

16. I made linking remarks

17. I was sensitive to the feelings of others

18. I respected minority opinion.

19. I expected the group concensus to be wiser than my opinion.

20. I helped the group to formulate its conclusions

21. I helped the group to formulate its plan of action

22. I had no hidden agenda

23. I listened deeply to persons I disagreed with

24. I avoided seizing the leadership of the group

Paul M. Miller is professor in the Church and Ministries Department at Associated Mennonite Biblical Seminaries, Elkhart, Indiana. He teaches courses in pastoral counseling, group leadership and group dynamics, pastoral leadership, and clinical pastoral education.

He holds ThD and ThM degrees from Southern Baptist Theological Seminary, BD and ThB degrees from Goshen Biblical Seminary, and the BA degree from Goshen College.

Reared in Lancaster County, Pennsylvania, he owned and managed a herd of purebred Holstein cattle and operated two farms for eight years. At 31 years of age he began training for a pastoral or missionary ministry.

Miller pastored a congregation for eight years, served as bishop of five congregations for twelve years, researched theological education in East Africa for two years, and served four months in Southern Africa in 1977.

He is author of *Peer Counseling in the Church* (Herald Press, 1978), *The Devil Did Not Make Me Do It* (Herald Press, 1977), *Equipping for Ministry in East Africa* (Central Tanganyika Press/

Herald Press, 1969), *Servant of God's Servants* (Herald Press, 1960), and *Group Dynamics in Evangelism* (Herald Press, 1954).

He is a supervisor in the Association of Clinical Pastoral Education and holds membership in the Christian Association for Psychological Studies locally. He is a member of the Belmont Mennonite Church, a congregation of the Mennonite Church in North America.

Miller has served as chaplain and trainer of chaplains in three hospitals, as a counselor to persons released from therapy to aid in their reentry into congregational life, and as a consultant and facilitator for numerous marriage enrichment seminars, couples' communication groups, renewal retreats, growth institutes, and group dynamic laboratories.

He is married to the former Bertha S. Mumma. They are the parents of four grown children.